THE GLOBAL PEACE PLAN
PART I

THE
INTERNATIONAL
DEMOCRATIC STANDARDS

WORLDWIDE DEMOCRACY
WITHOUT LOSS OF LIFE

RICARDO OSORIO, SR.

iUniverse, Inc.
NEW YORK   BLOOMINGTON

The Global Peace Plan Part I
The International Democratic Standards
Worldwide Democracy Without Loss of Life

iUniverse books may be ordered through booksellers or by contacting:

iUniverse
1663 Liberty Drive
Bloomington, IN 47403
www.iuniverse.com
1-800-Authors (1-800-288-4677)

Because of the dynamic nature of the Internet, any Web addresses or links contained in this book may have changed since publication and may no longer be valid.

ISBN: 978-1-4401-3154-7 (pbk)
ISBN: 978-1-4401-3155-4 (ebk)

Printed in the United States of America

iUniverse rev. date: 3/24/2009

Also by

Ricardo Osorio, Sr.

<u>Stop Worldwide Government Insanity</u>

ISBN: 0-595- 23126-8

Democracy is our ideal.

What is in question is the format that supports this concept.

Dedication:

In memory and profound respect to all men and women who fought to bring us democracy as we know it today, and those, whom at this moment, are still fighting for the countries living in darkness...

R.O., Sr.

This great planet and its people deserve a first class world political organization.

The Global Peace Plan presents to humanity simple decisive steps toward peacefully reaching this goal in less than 90 days.

CONTENTS

INTRODUCTION

- The objective of the Global Peace Plan is to present viable effortless solutions; simple steps that will not only eliminate the present grave political insurgency situation forever, but will finish the job of the American and French Revolutions on a worldwide basis.

- The Global Peace Plan creates the necessary basic scenery to vest all citizens in the world with sovereignty, freedom, and human rights.

- The intent and only purpose of this manuscript is to direct civilizations and their government representatives to exercise those options already available in order to reach Total Global Freedom.

- At this time, mankind has the momentum and by far the advantage, intellect, know-how, advanced technology, technical support, and all the vast global resources at its disposal to face any threat large or small.

- Worldwide governments have been in place at the global, continental, and national levels for the last fifty years.

- The record shows that the Charter of the United Nations, the Declaration of Universal Human Rights, and international global laws have been formulated and approved for all nations.

- We are in the most advantageous strategic world government position in our entire history.

- The upgraded worldwide democratic format in the Global Peace Plan will satisfy all democratic points of view.

- The democracy established will guarantee freedom and human rights for all.

- It will be in the best interest of humanity and democracy to think globally and to organize governments based on international democratic standards to work even better than the private sector.

- The United Nations, continental organizations, nations, states, counties, districts, and cities all over the world will enjoy peace and prosperity determined by specific long and short term master plans of their own.

  - The time has come to call on humanity and their legitimate government representative officials to combine efforts to make sure that the tragic events in our government's system in the past will not be repeated.

  - Small unscrupulous bands of criminal minds posing as or impersonating legitimate government officials are in every sense the worst dictators ever in the world. This 'Axis of Evil' and their accomplices not only keep their citizens in jail in their own countries but threaten the civilized world with a vast insurgency that goes from crimes against humanity to blackmail and threats to use nuclear arms, intercontinental missiles and biological agents in a diabolical plan to destroy the civilized world.

  - Due to the fact that the motivations of this global insurgency are to force mankind to do things "we the people" do not intend to do, leaves civilizations no other choice but to stand up and fight for our rights.

- Humanity using the Global Peace Plan and a new global government format will be certain this time that such treacherous behavior never occurs again.

- We want the democracy concept as our ideal to always prevail all over the world supported by more responsible governments that will rise to the occasion and justify their existence to meet our needs and that of the environment.

R.O., Sr.

CHAPTER I

THE POLITICAL PROBLEM:
THE EXISTING GLOBAL POLITICAL TRAGEDY

- Centuries of weak governments have left a legacy of total chaos in all nations.

- The history of humanity shows generation after generation, without exception, paying an incredible price in our struggle for true democracy.

- This humanity record shows not only worldwide government insanity, but also the tremendous magnitude of a problem for which a solution is long overdue.

- The purpose of this manuscript is to present a realistic and quick, viable solution with specifics, indisputable principles, and a new way of thinking; not trying to fight force with force, but to fight force with intellect.

  History will show that the present generation is living the bloodiest century in history.

O YEARS 400-500

Barbarian Invasions

These years were a time of terror, when the Huns under Attila moved across Asia and Europe killing people. It was an era

1

when men and women killed themselves rather than living and facing such horrible fights.

O YEARS 1750-1800

American Revolution and French Revolution ideals spread.

O YEARS 1800 to 2000 plus

The ideals, political documents and institutions formed by the American and French Revolutions represent a universal democratic reality today. The following have been approved by six billion people as a way of life:

> United Nations
> Seven continental organizations
> Confederations of 194 nations
> The United Nations Charter & Universal Declaration of
> Human Rights

The time has come to finish the work of the American and French revolutions. Freedom and democratic ideals were as close as any time in history to mastering a total politically civilized world.

The Global Peace Plan's five simple resolutions will lead humanity to finish that work.

PRESENT GLOBAL FORMAT STRONG POINTS

The United Nations (U.N.)

The present global format has existed since the opening of the United Nations in October, 1945. The United Nations has been established as an indisputable worldwide political organization.

Since its activation, the United Nations has set a precedent as a global forum for all nations of the world.

The Charter of the United Nations

"We the Peoples of the United Nations - United for a Better World," a brilliant document, subscribes to the idea of freedom, human rights and the policy of peace and prosperity among nations.

This document has been signed and approved by all member nations and applies to all six billion men and women on earth.

The International Court of Justice (World Court) is the main court to settle disputes among nations.

There are other U.N. organizations such as the:

General Assembly Secretariat

Security Council Economic and Social Council

In addition, there are another twenty specialized related agencies.

Major Continental International Organizations

African Union (AU)

The AU was established in 2002 and confirmed by 53 African nations with the main objective to focus on socio-economic matters and to bring peace and unity among their member states.

Headquarters: Ethiopia

Website: http://www.africa-union.org/

Asia-Pacific Economic-Cooperation (APEC)
APEC was founded in 1989 and serves as a forum to further cooperation on trade and investment between nations of the region and the rest of the world.

Headquarters: Singapore

Website: http://www.apec.org/

European Union (EU)

The main goal of the EU is to form an integrated economic, social and political union.

Headquarters: Brussels, Belgium

Website: http://europa.eu/

Organization of American States (OAS)

OAS was founded in Bogotá, Columbia in 1948 to promote an order of peace and justice on the America Continent.

Headquarters: Washington D.C.

Website: http://www.oas.org/

In addition, other continental organizations around the globe providing cooperation and development among nations and continents include the:

- International Criminal Court (ICC)
- Geneva Convention
- Commonwealth
- Caribbean Community and Common Market (CARICOM)
- North Atlantic Treaty Organization (NATO)

- Organization for Economic Cooperation and Development (OECD)
- Nations

There are 194 nations as part of this great confederation of nations.

All nations are well established with their own form of government.

All have constitutions in one way or another founded on the principles of freedom and human rights. There is not a threat or ambition of any civilized nation to take over another nation small or large. Totalitarian governments have been altering the spirit of their constitutions for political gains with the goal of remaining in power indefinitely.

Strong global trade exists between nations of all countries.

Summary:

Major Global Organizations:

- 40 Major Global and Continental Organizations
- Governments in all Nations

Total Cost to "We the People" in Dollars:

Humanity's support of the political global budget is in excess of trillions of dollars annually to maintain all governments and almost half is spent on security for the military to fight dictators and the global insurgency.

Present Global Format

Weak Points:

The United Nations, continental organizations and the 194 nations have been notorious for their lack of managerial skills to take care of business for humanity and the maintenance of the planet Earth.

The following are the most outstanding major mistakes of the present global organization since 1945 until the present time:

- Missing a great opportunity in 1989 and the 1990s to establish a worldwide democratic system at the fall of the Soviet Union. It was the moment to call for full freedom all over the world.
- Consenting to the illegal forceful takeover of nations by dictators and their accomplices.

This broke a major rule of the constitution of those nations, continental organizations, and the United Nations Charter.

It was in violation of the most sacred laws of Mother Nature and the Laws of Decency given as the birthright of freedom to all men and women.

- This was a loss of the constitutional sovereignty of "we the people," freedom, human rights, freedom of the press, right to assemble, and the choice to elect government officials. Instead, citizens all over the world watch as elections are stolen.

As a result, humanity faces a global insurgency promoted by the return of an 'Axis of Evil' in 19 nations with the worst dictators ever in the history of the earth.

At the close of the 1990s and the opening of the 2000s, due to mistakes by the present political system, humanity is living in a satanic world at the present time.

- Genocides
- The bombing of cities and the killing of thousands of innocent people around the world.

- The instability of the global economies.
- The manipulations of the oil price-per-barrel, causing disruption of values in all basic products consumed by humanity.

The Global Peace Plan's policies are very simple:

- To bury more than two thousand years of deadly global political past and be certain this treacherous behavior never again endangers humanity.
- To open a new worldwide political democratic system that will work better than the private sector; satisfying all points of view while preserving the government.

WE FACE THE FOLLOWING PROBLEM:

Worldwide Insurgency Front Composed of 19 Dictators and their Accomplices

The Return of the 'Axis of Evil'

The 19 Dictators and their accomplices, representing the 'Axis of Evil', are without a shadow of a doubt, in violation of the universal democratic systems of values of democracy and international laws.

They masquerade, pretend, pose, and authorize themselves by brutal force as legitimate representatives of a country contrary to the rules of law of the Charter of the United Nations, Universal Declaration of Human Rights, the Organization of American States, European Union, African Union, Oceanic Union, Asian Union and the confederations of nations.

Above all they are in violation of the major rules of humanity:
- Freedom
- Human rights

- Right to assemble
- Freedom of the Press

The Return of the 'Axis of Evil' - The Worldwide Worst Dictators

The most dangerous people in the world, composed of only 19 people and their accomplices, are in every sense the archenemies of civilization.

Their aim is to disable civilization and freedom using:

- Oil
- Bloodshed
- Drugs
- Counterfeit Currency
- Threat of nuclear arms
- Sabotaging international laws
- Adversely adjusting the constitutions to their own nations

They use any means, legal or illegal, to secure their positions.

How can only 19 people take over nations by force and intimidate the civilized world?

What is questionable is that no one supports such people. They are troublemakers, affecting all men and women on this planet.

Present 'Axis of Evil' in the 2000s:

Asia:

1.	Hu Jintao	China
2.	Kim Jong II	North Korea
3.	Than Shwe	Burma
4.	Saparmurat Niyazov	Turkmenistan
5.	Mahmoudud Ahmadinejad	Iran

6. Islam Karimov   Uzbekistan
7. Bashar al-Assad   Syria
8. Boungnang Vorachith   Laos
9. Dmitri Medvedev-Vladimir Putin Russia
   partnership

Europe:

1. Alekandr Lukashenco   Belarus

Africa

1. Omar al-Bashir   Sudan
2. Robert Mugabe   Zimbabwe
3. King Abdullah   Saudi Arabia
4. Teodoro Obiang Nguema   Guinea
5. Muammar al-Qaddafi   Libya
6. Meles Zenawi   Ethiopia
7. King Mswatt III   Swaziland
8. Isayas Afewerki   Eritrea

America:

The Castro brothers   Cuba

The Present Global Political Danger

The Vast Global Conspiracy

Chinese and Russian Connection

The World Political Inferno:

The oppressive Chinese and Russian regimes are in pursuit of world dominance. They believe that using force, guerrilla warfare, ideologies, and sabotaging our worldwide political system will satisfy their delusions of grandeur to conquer the world for the purpose of dividing it between them.

Their intentions and actions in all aspects of their domestic and foreign affairs are well known and documented.

The innocent Chinese and Russian people have been victimized for centuries by illegitimate governments and their leaders imposing their communist ideologies on them.

These innocent people are unaware that their own existence is in danger due to the war games that threaten the civilized world and could spark a nuclear war.

Unscrupulous dictators and their accomplices have come to believe that by using other countries under totalitarian regimes as puppets they can extend their influence and promote insurgencies on all continents.

The Chinese and Russian governments provide financial resources and military weapons, advisors, missile capabilities, and intelligence reports to nations like North Korea, Cuba, Iran, and Syria.

These oppressive governments in turn use the resources to finance and support insurgencies with the purpose of promoting global terror.

In the last fifteen years, China has increased its military capability to such a magnitude that the free world questions their intentions.

The Chinese military has extended their terror by going into space and hitting satellites causing unnecessary debris and concern about these capabilities. They have done this to interfere and destroy satellites for the purpose of blackmailing civilization.

Russia managed to cut the oil supply to former Eastern European nations causing a threat to those countries to keep their independence.

Russia openly supports and delivers nuclear capabilities to Iran even over the objections of the United Nations.

The present dictator of Russia, President Vladimir Putin, ignores all the efforts of citizens to fight the Nazis only to find themselves governed by a former KGB agent doing such things as poisoning opponents in Eastern European nations, newspaper men and women, or any who interfere in Putin's desire to extend Russian power and keep himself in power indefinitely.

The voting of President Putin for a second term with less than 70% of the population is being questioned by international observers because of undemocratic procedures which were believed to have been used. Recently Putin has arranged for his protégé to run for President in order to maintain his power.

- It is very clear that the illegal governments of China and Russia intentionally and maliciously have plotted against the civilized world and their institutions.

- The Chinese and Russian delegations to the United Nations veto any effort or intent to reach peace and prosperity in the world.

- On the American continent, the totalitarian Cuban government is a Chinese and Russian central command interference used to openly destroy the democratic process in the western hemisphere.

- The Chinese and Russians use the same tactics by constantly directing their far left followers to divide the American continent and support political leaders with communist ideologies to be elected in tainted elections with the only intent to isolate the United States and Canada politically and economically from the rest of the continent.

- Mexico is a perfect example of domestic and foreign interference in their elections. Freedom was tainted in the last elections by brainwashing Mexican voters to elect left wing candidates. Because of this, at the present moment the entire nation is in major turmoil with crime and illicit drug trafficking of major proportions weakening the present democratic elements of Mexican government.

- The African continental nations are in turmoil because of the constant interference of dictators to abolish freedom and democratic governments.

- The Philippine nation finds itself in a daily assault by a terrorist organization.

- The Lebanese government is in its own way being controlled by a strong terrorist organization supported by the illegitimate government of Iran and the dictator of Syria who openly give money to demonstrators and cause problems for the legitimate government of Lebanon.

- Iraq, in its struggle for democracy after a high percentage of its people voted for a new constitution and selected their democratic government, found themselves in the center of the most criminal terrorist group that the human race has seen since Attila the Hun.

- Iran and Syria are involved to prevent, at all costs, the progress of their people to have a democracy.

- A multinational force of 26 is in the Iraqi area to support the Iraqi military forces in the fight against the terrorists.

- Chinese missiles violated Japanese air space with the intent of intimidating Japan.

Citizens of the world: If you think that the present 19 dictators in the world today will be the last of our global problems, **think again**.

A. Illicit Drug Cartels

- Cartels in Afghanistan and Colombia exist presently at such magnitudes that these two nations that have worked hard to try to keep their fragile democracy at all costs, find themselves under deadly assault by these terrorist organizations.

- One half of Colombia has been taken over by the most dangerous guerrilla organizations ever imagined.

- Afghanistan has one of the most suffering peoples in the world as they struggle for peace and prosperity. They have finally set the tone for their democratic establishment. By doing that, they find themselves in the middle of combined illicit drug trafficking groups and the Taliban insurgency war. At the present time, a full deployment of NATO forces is in this nation in support of the Afghanistan democratic government.

B. Foreign Terrorist Organizations

There are presently 41 Foreign Terrorist Organizations designated as FTOs.

This type of criminal organization started in the 1960s with the "Shining Path" in Peru with only 300 insurgents.

- Their activities are mostly devoted to building communist regimes and attacking political enemies.
- They claim to have assassinated 30,000 people by bombing and assaulting villages.

The Shining Path has gone from less than several hundred to the strength of 12,000 in Colombia, and now deal in drug trafficking, kidnapping, and guerrilla warfare.

Most dictators harbor and support their FTO's training and supply them with arms. These 41 terrorist organizations have infiltrated all continents with different names and a diversity of purposes.

This insurgency involves criminal suicide-bombing, beheading of people, hijacking airliners, car bombing, taking foreign people hostage, murdering journalists, rocket attacks, attacking diplomats, and bombing tourist facilities. They have launched attacks on Casablanca, France, Israel, London, Madrid, New York, and foreign military bases. They have bombed embassies and carried out major terrorist acts in Iraq including mortar attacks on coalition forces in Afghanistan and Iraq, guerrilla warfare, bank robberies, and drug trafficking.

All these organizations are archenemies of freedom and democracy. At present, 19 dictators including China and Russia have never supported freedom, human rights, or democracy as a universal system of values and never will.

Characteristics of a Dictator

- Less educated than the average person in their country
- Never held a job
- Incapable of surviving in the civilized world
- Clueless about money
- Usually get in power by criminal behavior
- Find politics as the only way to survive
- Claim to defend the poor as a way to stay in power
- Dislike and mistrust industrialized nations
- Suppress freedom and the media
- Preach humility but live luxuriously
- Deposit millions of dollars in foreign banks
- Have an army of body guards to protect them
- Always change their sleeping routine
- Have people test their food
- Remain in power at all costs

All of them leave a path of misery and tragedy.

Global Unending Crime Scene

It has been a puzzle for humanity that this calamity has been going on for so long. For more than two millenniums, events such as global, continental, and regional wars have shaken the world. In fact, there is not a piece of land on this planet that has not seen a battle or fight. The intent of the dictators and their accomplices is to destroy our culture and civilization that so slowly and painfully we have built. Horrible acts of terror are still going on today with no end in sight.

- We start in the year 400 A.D. with the barbarian invasions of the Hun, led by Attila, going across the desert to the Asia and European continents committing acts of terrorism.
- Today we find ourselves threatened with the same diabolic criminal mind, the killing of men, women, and innocent children. It is very simple: we are still living back in the Dark Ages.

To make matters worse, terrorists today use weapons of mass destruction and systematic vast subversion; always using the darkness to plan the next assault, with legal or illegal tactics to kill or torture. Kidnapping, massacres, and bombings are carried out; and then terrorists use the free press to take credit and intimidate the civilized world.

Greatest Missed Global Opportunities in History for World Peace:

Generation after generation, in the last 2000 years we have reached moments where the political opportunities were presented to bring a truly worldwide global democracy.

First Global Turning Point in History: 1776

In the year 1776, the American and French Revolutions took place. These events ignited the world to the idea of forming democracies. The new ideal of democracy spread in some nations and many countries gained independence.

Second Global Turning Point in History: 1945

During World War II, the whole world was shocked with the magnitude of incredible disasters where the continent of Europe was left practically in ruins. The loss of lives reached the highest level ever with more than 60,000,000 people killed. Political leaders during that time conceived the idea of a United Nations, established in October, 1945; a place where all nations' members could resolve practically any problem in a "civilized forum."

Third Global Turning Point in History: 1989

In our time, it was with great significance that the Berlin Wall was brought down along with the collapse of the communistic philosophy; the most feared ideology. It was a victory for a civilized world of major proportions. The year 1989 ignited jubilee as an excellent opportunity for a worldwide democracy.

To the disbelief of the entire free world, once again, political leaders missed a golden opportunity to bring freedom to the whole world. The United Nations and leaders at that time missed an opportunity to present a plan for a universal democratic system of values attached to the Charter of the United Nations to present a new way of thinking where all governments will run the business of "we the people" even better than does their industry.

These misjudgments are unacceptable and left most nations around the planet vulnerable and open for abuses under fragile democratic formats. The ever present 'Axis of Evil' nations made their move all over the world to open a new chapter in history; the return of the 'axis of evil.'

The 21ˢᵗ Century

EXTREMELY IMPORTANT MESSAGE

WARNING TO HUMANITY

The United Nations does not have a mechanism in place to enforce and guarantee democracy in all nations. As a result, "we the people," men and women all over the world are unprotected in terms of our basic freedom and human rights.

Observations:

- The United Nations has the obligation to protect freedom at all costs around the globe.
- It is unacceptable that at this moment 19 dictators and their accomplices keep their citizens in jail in their own nations and the rest of the world lives in a state of red alert when it is supposed to be the other way around.

Why We Have to Live in Constant Global Political Insanity:

At this very moment all of us six billion people are directly affected by a few unscrupulous dictators who keep themselves in power indefinitely by all legal or illegal means.

History has recorded conflict in all possible ways:

- insurgencies
- genocides
- bombings
- assassinations of political opponents
- illegal drug trafficking
- piracy on the high seas
- sabotaging voting results in democratic nations
- opposing freedom in the United Nations Security Council
- two major wars and the present global war insurgency
- Vietnam, North Korea, Gulf War, Iraq, Afghanistan, Lebanon, Israel-Palestine and Georgia-Russia in 2008

The dictators move to the next level of crime by using our own inventions like airplanes as projectile bombs against buildings and using these masterpieces of engineering in the killing of innocent men and women. Also, they have been involved in bombing cities, trains, restaurants, weddings, funerals, and churches. Their goal is to simply blow out civilization on our planet earth.

The 'Axis of Evil' are the ones behind all of these atrocities. They employ brainwashing of men, women, and children to irrationally become suicide bombers.

They are behind the overnight increase in the global price of oil, which affects the cost of living around the globe, thereby raising the price of all consumer products.

The political world leaders have been limited in their response and confine themselves to a small segment of the planet rather than seeing the big picture at a global level. Due to this narrow point of view, the system is open for abuse as dictators create major international conflicts at will. It gets to the point that war is the only way out.

This notion of a war mentality is nothing new. It has been with us for centuries as well as the 'axis of evil.'

Once again humanity is not in a position to ignore the present war of terror that affects our way of life by simply hoping that it will go away.

It affects all of us without exception. We will have to make some changes in our attitude to stop this present global insurgency. Is it not our moral obligation and debt of honor to all the freedom fighters and to us to support this struggle for worldwide freedom?

It is in the best interest of the poor, the middle class, the rich, the private sector, and government officials to recognize these present circumstances and respond accordingly. We have to stand up and fight for freedom and there are ways we can use our ingenuity to support these actions.

Humanity must subscribe to the idea that by combining the global free press, the worldwide political system, and all world resources at our disposal, represents the most powerful force system ever built on this planet.

The simple glamorization of this political concept alone will have immense psychological impact. When civilization is united and the constant terror nonsense of a small band of dictators and their accomplices is over, it will send a clear and powerful signal that this time civilization means business. The time has come for dictators and their accomplices to start packing or face the end of their lives like their counterparts Hitler, Mussolini, Saddam Hussein, Milosevic and all others charged with crimes against humanity. This time the penalty will not be simple political exile. All doors will be closed to them and there will be no place to harbor these dictators and their accomplices. Put simply, this will be the end of dictators, insurgencies, and the illicit drug trade from our history books.

We have to stop wasting time merely talking about it and instead begin building on all continents the greatest world opinion and global propaganda democratic machine against this criminal 'axis of evil.'

Ricardo Osorio, Sr.

Global Suggestions

Constructive Solutions

Concerns

Observations

CHAPTER II

To the Citizens of the World: The End of Substandard Governments Worldwide

- There are simple formulas that show how to successfully run organizations using proper procedures.

- These well recognized formulas constitute the missing link in our present worldwide governments.

- The organization and administration of humanity and the planet earth is considered the most delicate task in the world.

- The Global Peace Plan subscribes to the idea that logical and sound economic and democratic principles are the answer to support the democratic concept.

The Universal System

From the viewpoint of science, the universal system moves objects through the vastness of space following a program of directions for not only our solar system but also for similar star systems maintaining planet earth at a precise distance from the sun, thus providing the support mechanism in such a way that flora and fauna live over and over for billions of years. What is most amazing and unique is that it works all by itself. In short, it is a masterful system that works thanks to indisputable principles of physics.

B. The Global Industrial System

Industry and science have set unprecedented records in the last 75 years even under the present global, political unrest. Automobiles, airplanes, and appliances of all kinds represent some of these records. The computer, cell phones and the internet are all available to provide instant communication. In space, we have flown to the moon and built a space platform and launched space vehicles to reach other planets. Some major advances around the world include the building of bridges, skyscrapers, tunnels under the sea and dams. All were done with precise efficiency and completed in a short period of time. These major accomplishments of the human race are direct descendants of the universal system using intellectual curiosity and logical principals as tools to produce, in a variety of ways, these advanced products in all fields.

C. World Sport System

Humanity has put forward these unique principles to produce rules of law which enable mankind to watch the Olympic Games involving the finest athletes from all over the five continents coming together for competition. This shows what the human race can do when logical and common sense act together to set the tone for a common cause in organizations large or small.

D. Worldwide Government System

When it comes to the subject of government, humanity has for some reason based its approach on very primitive, immature, and limited procedures. On one hand, it can resolve very intricate problems of science but on the other seems unable to direct its destinies choosing instead to blindly follow ideologies, religions and often satanic leaders who offer only false hopes. The result is that the entire population has been led into misery, ignorance, and brutality. Primitive humanity started in the Dark Ages and some nations are still living there today. The magnitude of this problem is so great that on more than one occasion we have tried to destroy ourselves and diminish the planet earth's support system.

UNIVERSAL PROOF

The following specific facts show how universal, global and industrial organizations along with the Olympics use indisputable principles and the rule of law as the way to turn around any organization including present worldwide government organizations in a sound and efficient format that will enable humanity and the environment to excel:

A. The Universal System, P(1)

B. The Global Industrial System, P(2)

C. World Sport System, P(3)

D. Worldwide Government System, P(4)

A RATIONAL SCIENTIFIC PROOF

We note that the systems A through C operate, for the most part, harmoniously in an efficient manner for the benefit of all. However, system D has been broken for a very long time and has become dangerously chaotic. We assert that there exists a set of principles P(4) which will cause system D to operate as well as P(1), P(2), and P(3) do for systems A, B, and C, respectively.

For more than 2000 years, system D has attempted to survive in a combination of contradictory belief systems. Some ideologies, with religious and authoritative dictators, are bringing both confusion and a legacy of total chaos. We claim that there exists a set of fundamental principles P(4) in which system D will operate as well as systems A, B, and C.

The United Nations, their institutions, the seven continental organizations, and 194 confederations of nations have left us a legacy of negligence and poor decision making which has brought us to the point where system D has not been operating effectively due to using baseless foundations.

Indisputable principles such as P(1) through P(3) are as effective as a scientific proof.

Worldwide Democratic Government Empire Complex

What Humanity Wants

Mankind has successfully accomplished advances in all endeavors, but there is one which has been the longest and the hardest ever to overcome, which is the realization of a *worldwide government format* that will work better than the private sector and bring peace and prosperity to the world.

Humanity has to be prepared. We are inches away from accomplishing this dream. Generation after generation, including all who have paid a price with sacrifices, has brought us close to, not only freedom and human rights, but also the ability to master worldwide government organizations.

"We the people", united not divided, shall support the Global Peace Plan implementation along with the following organizations:

The United Nations
World Court
Global Trade Organization
World Bank
Organization of American States
European Union
African Union
All 194 nations
All political parties that represent democracies
Scientific organizations
Universities all over the world

Women's organizations
Environmental organizations
World free press, radio, world movie industry, and Internet users

Clubs or associations that support freedom should be prepared to assist in the successful transitional change to the greatest political event where humanity will enjoy the best of both worlds; the planet earth and a civilized world. This global effort calls for a serious commitment from all of us. The key to success requires a mutual unity to achieve the outcome humanity is seeking.

We, the people of the world, in order to conceive a worldwide administrative government format more suitable to the present time, see that secure peace and prosperity must be goal-oriented to score higher in efficiency, satisfy all points of view and preserve the environment by the establishment of a *worldwide democratic government empire complex*.

Criteria:

Due to the magnitude and complexity in administrating humanity and the maintenance of earth, it will be in the best interest to establish administrative levels of responsibility.

The three major global political organizations, Global Level, Continental Level and National Level will exercise power at their levels and will work together to carry out specific tasks and levels of responsibility.

The Worldwide Democratic Government Empire Complex will be structured as follows:

Global Level:

- Composed of the United Nations, the World Trade Organization and the World Court

Continental Level:

- Contains the seven continents and the appropriate continental organizations:

America   Organization of America States

Europe   European Union

Africa   African Union

Oceania   Oceanic Union

Asia   Asian Union

Arctic   United Nations Arctic Organization

Antarctic   United Nations Antarctic Organization

National Level:

- Involves the present confederations of nations composed of 194 nations.

Worldwide Democratic Government Empire Complex

"We the people," in order to form a more perfect world and establish freedom and justice for all men and women, promote peace and tranquility, and secure liberty and posterity for ourselves, do ordain the worldwide government empire complex.

ARTICLE 1

Section1

All three levels of government have separate powers but will work united to preserve peace and tranquility across the globe.

Section 2

All three levels of government will be separate but will act together to secure, defend, and protect the Charter of the United Nations, Universal Human Rights, and international democratic standards.

Section 3

The establishment of a major principle in the government system where all major levels of government in the world; the global level, continental level, and the national level exercise a check upon the actions of others. Checks and balances limit government's authority by pitting power against power.

Section 4

The establishment of a *global zero tolerance policy* that requires any large or small government agency to provide transparency, integrity, credibility, and adhering to the universal rule of law.

No state or person in the world is above the law.

Continental Level

The following continental organizations will be crucial to lead humanity to a more workable organization in the worldwide democratic government empire complex:

- The Organization of American States
- European Union
- African Union
- Asian union
- Oceanic Union
- United Nations Arctic Administration
- United Nations Antarctic Administration

The continental level will have the identical organization as does the United Nations due to the following reasons:

- Continental organizations will have the same responsibilities but at the continental level.
- It will be in the best interest of the worldwide democratic government empire complex to have unified organizations as well as standard procedures at both levels.

Manifesto

The Public Democratic Declaration of Political Interest

To the citizens of the world:

The Global Peace Plan has simple guidelines and decisive steps to move to the missing link that humanity has been looking for. The plan will help turn around the existing treacherous disorganized system toward a more credible global political organization.

"We the people" believe that the Global Peace Plan's intent and objective is not only to finish the job of the American and French Revolutions but eventually to prevent the collapse of a global politically weak organization.

Humanity has been searching in the political market for a quality global format that supports the democratic concept.

Our generation has called upon us to do our duty by sending a direct message to the global mass media and the present political establishment; to put aside all political differences with the idea of approving the beginning of a logical common sense approach for a common cause that eventually will lead to the end of government mediocrity.

It will be in the best interest of humanity and the planet earth to combine all efforts behind a new *global united policy* that puts the pressure of *world opinion* on the present political leaders to adopt this plan.

"We the people" understand the political lessons of the past and the present political tragedies. The facts speak for themselves. The ramifications of more than two centuries of global wars of incredible shocking and despicable global crimes against humanity are of biblical proportions to the point of human defamation.

 Once the entire European continent was destroyed and the following acts affected the entire globe:

- Genocides
- Insurgency
- Destruction of cities, hospitals, trains, airplanes, restaurants, offices buildings, religious monuments
- Beheading of men and women
- Poisoning and assassinations for political reasons
- Illicit drug traffic
- Killing of free press men and women

Citizens of the world, now is the time for all of us to be aware that it is our responsibility to make changes all over the world.

All of the above crimes against humanity are directly caused by a small band of dictators, posing and pretending to be heads of state, supported only by their accomplices. No reasonable person in the entire world should support these 19 totalitarian people and their accomplices.

Dictators use their national and global resources, including drug cartels, to finance and support dozens of insurgencies in all continents. This is done in poor and advanced nations using any legal or illegal interruptions of freedom, human rights, or political programs around the world.

The last vestiges of totalitarian governments belong to the Dark Ages. They must come to an end very quickly because at this very moment they intend to build nuclear arms in order to blackmail the free world.

There is no valid excuse, either legal or technical, for the United Nations, the five continental organizations, secretary generals, 194 heads of nations, and six billion people not to proceed and demand immediate eviction of this group of individuals with "Attila the Hun" attitudes and charge all of them with crimes against humanity.

A Preview and Global Report Card of our Future with a United Civilized
"Worldwide Government Democratic Empire Complex"

Men and women of the world:

We have come a long way thanks to more than two hundred million men and women who paid the ultimate devotional sacrifice to defend our freedom.

The Worldwide Government Democratic Empire Complex consists of:

- One planet earth
- Six billion people
- One United Nations and their institutions
- Seven continental organizations
- Confederations of 194 nations

The global legal report:

The entire global documentation must be approved by all nations that set the tone of advanced civilized society and rule by Universal laws:

- The Charter of the United Nations
- Universal Declaration of Human Rights

- World Court
- Continental Charter
- 194 nations constitutions

A global political finance report:

- Humanity spends trillions and trillions of dollars annually to support legal and illegal governments across the globe.
- More than half of this annual global budget is wasted by civilizations that, for the last two centuries, have been fighting brutal forces such as the present global insurgency that affects all continents.

Global industry complex report:

- In the last 75 years, humanity has amazed the world, even under politically unfavorable circumstances. This shows how civilized people as *united* men and women have been able to excel in disciplines such as mathematics, physics, engineering, and medicine. Some examples are automobiles built by robots, jet airplanes, the Internet, cell phones, the bar code, and all other products that benefit humanity today.

All of this shows how a free society working hard can solve complex problems like going to the moon and building a space platform.

The Present Generation's Global Political Job

The Global Peace Plan subscribes to the idea that the present substandard political organization can be improved by using available economic and democratic universal systems of values. It will build a worldwide government democratic complex to the highest levels of excellence that will work better than the private sector, thus satisfying the poor, middle class, and the rich in the economy of industry, government, and the planet earth.

The United Nations, Continental Organizations, and the Confederations of Nations

- It is the duty of the entire gubernatorial global system to protect, defend, and enforce existent global procedures approved by all nations.

- All government officials and their employees must stand up and defend the sovereign rights of men and women everywhere in the world, not the other way around.

- In the concept of values of any nation, freedom and human rights are paramount.

- Government officials are vested with the power to protect people who cannot defend themselves.

United Nations Resolutions

- After two centuries of work and sacrifices by humanity, the global political foundations exist to move to the next level.

- The global political organization is close to building a solid organization that will finish the job of the American and French Revolutions.

- All of humanity and the global mass media are ready to support our government officials on all continents by implementing the Global Peace Plan requirements.

The following five global resolutions are the keys for success and need to be implemented immediately:

1. Activation of consultative global task force
2. Total global freedom
3. Worldwide government democratic empire complex
4. Continental recovery master plan implementation.
5. United Nations Political Science Advance Institute

Successful National Administrations and their Companion Political Parties System:

The 194 Nations of the Future

It will be in the best interest of the present political party system to persuade nations, large or small, poor or rich to establish their own specific *national master plan agenda* that realistically addresses the domestic and foreign issues of their country.

A *national master plan agenda* is a mix of economic and democratic principles of long and short term values that will drive all nations, regardless of their status, into a much better socioeconomic, industrial, governmental, and environmental position. The plan will be organized to build and support strong confederations of nations in a new direction and into a political structure more sustainable in the present time. It will be a move to lead all nations to become successful prototypes of a pilot model for other nations to emulate and rank high in the global standard of living.

The plan will produce a quality of government remarkably simple in its policies in education, housing, pension plans, health care and senior citizen care. A simple tax procedure and a strong banking system along with environmental controls and the right to make a living by both genders will be an uninterrupted system that will make detail changes or adjustments only at election time.

Under this concept, a combination of the above with good managerial skills will lead naturally to a proper economy and to a higher level of industrial excellence.

All of these components plus high managerial skills in the proper economy will be the tipping point to enable all nations, poor or rich to excel as well as any other in the confederations of nations. In contrast to the above, the existing weak democratic format, as we know it, has been used throughout time by ideologies in an effort to create illusions and false hopes to bring "we the people" under their control.

Simple Steps for a Successful Group of Nations and Their Political Party System:

The administration of a nation's states, counties, districts, and cities is without question the most sensitive task mankind ever encounters. Political parties can play a very important role in the life of nations all over the world. The party system errors in the last centuries can be corrected and used as a history lesson by bringing into the present a democratic system with two fundamental principles VOICE POWER and VOTE POWER of the people that have been missing in the administration of nations.

Humanity never visualized that the world would turn around many times before the *vote power* would be sufficient to keep governments in perspective, but time proves the contrary. More than the *vote* alone, *voice power* was needed and was equally important. Lack of voice power became one of the greatest faults of the democratic system. If from the beginning of time men and women had equally balanced the exercise of voice and vote power in a democratic format to direct their destiny, the history of humanity would be quite different.

Humanity has never given itself a chance to master a *true global democratic system*. The present political global system has been unsuccessful due to the favoring of special interests or by confining thinking to a single region rather than capturing comprehension of the entire planet.

The Global Peace Plan converts all of that abuse in specific and indisputable democratic and economic principles of today that will end humanity's struggle for a true democratic system in every single nation all over the world.

Voice and Vote Power are the Most Powerful Tools that Freedom has ever Created.

WARNING:

The United Nations, continental organizations, 194 nations, and their political parties that represent six billion people have now, more than ever, the responsibility to defend and protect humanity by eliminating the present weak global organization that adversely affects all continents. It is imperative that this be corrected in order to protect civilization from abuses and remove the opportunity for failure. It is impossible for government to run the business of the people without a long and short term master plan and the proper hiring of personnel for the most sensitive jobs in the world.

The Confederations of Nations:

Implementation of the following independent agencies in all 194 nations:

- The National Independent Research Master Plan Agency
- The National Independent Electoral Agency

These agencies will be implemented by an executive order from their own government. They will be independent and at the cabinet level. Under no circumstances will these agencies be under the government's control. They will be composed of fifteen boards of directors, consisting of the most brilliant men and women available, with long academic and industrial backgrounds and strict job qualifications.

The National Independent Research Master Plan Agency:

The Voice Power of "We the People"

The nations will protect the voice power of the people.

The National Independent Research Master Agency will develop a 100 year master plan for all domestic and foreign issues concerning the future of the nation. The master plan will provide long and short term sophisticated and analytical programs.

1. The master plan will make public its findings and facts in a simple format, so all will be able to understand. This will be done by highlighting all the national issues during each election.
2. The agency will issue a three option version of the national master plan with the intention that all citizens will exercise voice power, via ballot.
3. The agency will make corrections after the plan has been screened and debated by the candidates running for office.
4. Long term, as well as short term goals, will be required to ensure that the nation continuously keeps pace with all the national issues: social, economic, government, environmental, and beatification in the best national interest.
5. The agency will make certain every national issue is scrutinized by the best team of experts who, above all, will choose the best course of action for the country.
6. The agency will issue to the congress the 100 year master plan chosen by the people at inauguration time.
7. Every quarter, the agency will make public the status of the nation and the progress of the nation's 100 year master plan. It will make public a *national report card* in the business section of the newspapers concerning the status of social, economic, government, environmental, and beatification. The national report card will itemize the peoples' concerns with comments and suggestions in general. The report will include necessary statistical charts, graphics, and visual aids in plain language easy to understand by the average citizen.
8. The national report card will reflect a summary of the progress of the nation each quarter in the same manner as is used by the nation's industry. This quarterly progress is compared with last year's expectations for the next quarter.

The 100 year master plan, as well as short term goals, will be appropriate to ensure that nations continually keep pace with the issues in the best national interest and be updated for the next election period.

The National Independent Electoral Agency: The Vote Power of the People

This agency will protect the vote power of the people and it will have the following duties:

1. The agency will promote a policy developed by the best qualified personnel in political sciences.
2. The agency will set the nation's jobs application requirements and distribute them to the appropriate government agencies. All efforts will be focused on acquiring the best minds with the intent to obtain optimum results in the government.
3. The national campaign time will be reduced to four months; a period starting August 15th and ending December 15th. It will have a mega election format.
4. The national government jobs will command salaries equal to or better than those in the industry counterpart.
5. Any government personnel proven to act contrary to his/her duties will step aside immediately and will be prosecuted to the fullest extent of the law. Those individuals will never work in the public sector again.
6. **The national state elections format** – Each state in the union will present to the nation their candidate for president, vice-president, congressmen, governor, and heads of counties, districts, and cities in a national mega election.
7. All public officials will be required by law to pass a government aptitude test to show that they are familiar with the nation's 100 year master plan's domestic and foreign issues. They will have to be familiar with government procedures at every level including the United Nations, continental organizations, federal, state, county, district, and city.
8. The election system of all nations will be in accordance with the seal of approval of the United Nations, the Organization of American States, the European Union, the African Union,

the Asian Union, the Oceanic Union and the confederations of nations.

9. As a precautionary measure, nations which are new to the free world will experiment with one term in four years at a time rather than the traditional senior democratic nation's restriction to two consecutive terms only.

All nations, rich or poor, will be a competitor in their own field of expertise such as agriculture, industry, sciences, technology, tourism, environment, or a combination of all.

Oil nations that generate a vast fortune have the advantage and opportunity. They can develop at an accelerated rate to direct all efforts in a master plan to be goal oriented and rely on a back-up plan when the time comes that the oil sources are no longer needed or superimposed by other means.

The 100 year master plan is applicable at the global political level such as the United Nations, the continental organizations, the Organizations of American States, the European Union, the African Union, the Asian States, the Oceanic Union, the Arctic and the Antarctic continents.

The European Union is a perfect example for other continents to follow. They have accomplished harmony and strong political stability in a short time. The Euro, as sole currency, is one of the major achievements of the European Union. There is no excuse. Other continents need to follow the simple steps of the European Union as demonstrated by the continent of Europe.

Global Suggestions

Constructive Solutions

Concerns

Observations

CHAPTER III

The International Democratic Standards: We the People, United We Stand

Worldwide Government Democratic Empire Complex

The International Democratic Standards

Content:

- We the People Resolution
- We the People Declaration
- 24 Amendments

We the People Resolution:

At the present time, the confederations of nations, the United Nations, and continental multinational organizations lead us to believe that this binding trust between "we the people" and the present government relationship will eventually lead to a civilized world; but to the contrary, the facts speak for themselves. Governments just closed the bloodiest century in history.

At the start of the new millennium, "we the people" find ourselves in fear of global and bio-terrorist warfare. It has killed thousands of people through madness and faceless terrorism which has shocked the already fragile global economy.

All nations and the United Nations do not have a viable mechanism to balance our social, economic, government, industrial, environmental, beautification, and foreign and domestic policies as is required by the power vested in all of us.

Therefore, "we the people" resolve to direct the confederations of nations, the United Nations and continental organizations to produce a clear democratic format on an upgraded prototype government in 90 days.

The International Democratic Standards Declaration

"We the people," empowered by the heritage inherent in all of us, the universal forces, natural laws, and the laws of decency unanimously choose as an ultimatum, the Global Peace Plan.

"The democratic concept" is our ideal and our way of life. We choose to be supported by indisputable principles and rules in an upgraded government format superior to industry efficiency. We must attain our sacred right of life in a new prototype government. It must, without exception, have standards, principles, and rules applicable to all nations and multinational governments. This will be designated in such a manner as to represent all points of view, satisfying the poor, the middle class, the rich, industry, and also important environmental issues.

Amendments

"We the people" of all nations, in order to form a more perfect confederations of nations, the United Nations, and continental organizations, must establish international democratic standards; common principles and rules to secure our freedom with justice, domestic tranquility and harmony.

We must establish the following amendments to be included in all levels of government:

Amendment I

"We the people," vested as the ultimate authority, in order to form a more perfect confederations of nations, securing the blessings of liberty to ourselves and our descendents, do ordain that the time has come to establish that all nations be governed by "international democratic standards" as a common ground.

Amendment II

All Men and Women are Created Equal

Amendment III

All nations and continental organizations of the free world shall have equal standing before the United Nations.

Amendment IV

Independent Research Agency

The function of the independent research agency is to assist the United Nations, continental groups, nations, states, districts, and cities to have a mechanism in place to direct these organizations to achieve calculated goals in a continuous 100 year master plan. This plan is in regards to social, economic, government, industrial, environmental and beautification issues in order to achieve optimum results.

Section 1

Formation of a working business relationship between "we the people" exercising our "voice power" with the independent research agency.

Section 2

"We the people" at election time will produce three versions of the 100 year master plan; A, B, or C.

Section 3

The independent research agency will be composed of highly skilled men and women and an independent board of directors at the cabinet level, but not under the executive branch.

Amendment V

Mega Election

"We the people" in all nations, the United Nations, continental, states, counties, districts, and cities will exercise, in a mega election, our voice and vote power.

Section 1

Voice power - Selecting either plan A, B, or C as the best suitable 100 year master plan to satisfy social, economic, government, industrial, environmental, beautification, and domestic and foreign policy issues.

Section 2

Vote Power - Selecting highly qualified people who excel in the execution of the 100 year master plan of "We the people's" choice.

Amendment VI

Section 1

Requirement for public government officials:

All positions, without exception, from entry level to the upper echelon will be required to have qualifications superior to or above the average industry counterpart. "We the people" demand impeccable resumes at all times.

Section 2

Salaries

Public government officials all over the world at the entry level and upper echelon level in the United Nations, continental, nations, states or providences, counties, districts, cities or town level will have higher salaries than industry.

Section 3

Government Efficiency

Government officials in the United Nations and continental levels are required to maintain the quality of governmental institutions. This will be measured using a remarkably simple efficient system requiring scoring higher than industry to create the balance of social, economic, government, environmental, and beautification issues at all times in governments all over the world.

Section 4

Government Report Card

The independent research agency will issue a quarterly report card based on efficiency in the same manner as industry. The independent research agency will publish the findings in the business section of newspapers.

Government report cards will be graded as follows:

- A - Excellent
- B - Passing

- C - Unacceptable

Section 5

WARNING

Public Government Officials and their Efficiency Report Card:

First C report card: warning will be issued.

Second C report card: dismissed immediately (without pay)

Public government official on conduct report card with any C report card: will result in administrative leave immediately (with pay until courts prove the contrary).

Public officials with a dishonorable discharge are prohibited from holding public office for life.

Amendment VII

Separation of Church and State in All Nations

Amendment VIII

National pension and health care plan in all nations

Section 1

All nations, without exception, must co-own both systems:

- National pension plan – governments will issue a supplement check to seniors or disabled citizens unable to live above the poverty line.
- National health plan – governments will provide the best medical care affordable in the world to all citizens, without exception. Citizens will contribute to the plan. The health plan

will be a profitable business co-owned by the government. It will be a system that satisfies the doctors, technical personnel, medical industry, and the citizens. The system will supply, at no cost, prescriptions to seniors and disabled people living under the poverty line.

Amendment IX

United Nations Independent Political Science Advance Institute

Section 1

The United Nations Independent Political Science Advance Institute will be created with the objective to teach government officials efficient managerial skills superior to those of industry.

Section 2

Standardize upscale government format to have a mix of democratic and industrial principles at all levels in the 194 nations including the United Nations and continental organizations.

Amendment X

All governments at any level must be structured under a 100 year master plan, updated every election.

Amendment XI

Election State or Providence-style Format

Section 1

All states or providences present their candidates to the nation

Amendment XII

Satellite Town Forum

All levels of government from the United Nations, nations, states or providences, countries, counties, districts, and cities by law will conduct "we the people" forum satellite town meeting at the end of every quarter, six months, and the end of the year, via direct participation by "we the people."

Amendment XIII

Federal election commission in all nations

Section 1

All federal election commissions will be independent.

Section 2

Under no circumstances will the election commissions be under government control.

Section 3

Elections will take place simultaneously in all confederations of nations, continental, and the United Nations by December 15 every four years.

Section 4

Due to the short period of campaign time, August 15th through December 15th, "we the people" will finance the whole process. Under no circumstances will political officials or their employees collect or accept extra remunerations. Democracy is not for sale. Any such violations will be considered a major crime against their nation.

Section 5

For a period of four years all government officials and institutes will be graded similarly to industry in conduct, efficiency, and goals to be achieved in the issues of social, economic, government, industrial, environmental, beautification, and domestic and foreign policy issues.

Section 6

There will be a separation of powers in all democratic institutions. As an example, heads of the branches, the President, Speaker of the House, and the Chief Supreme Court Justice will be separate but solely responsible before "we the people" for the efficiency of the government branches. The same rules will be applicable to states, counties, districts, and city institutions all over the world. All government institutions will be coordinated efficiently to attain optimum results quickly.

Section 7

"We the people" will demand that the Global Peace Plan be in place in all nations, the United Nations, and continental government organizations in order to lead the world to greatness.

Amendment XIV

City Civic Resident Volunteer Organization

City or town civic resident volunteer organizations are the key for successfully representing all points of view; all levels of income, all ways of life, the homeless, poor, middle class, upper class, industry, environmental, and beautification of the city.

Section 1

City civic resident volunteer organizations will work side by side with the city or town government like the homeowners' association concept but expanded to the level of city or town which not only protects the basic family unit association, but covers all the city territory and all men and women.

Section 2

A city where all of the residents will be participants with one common goal, one common denominator, one common concern: **their** city. Residents, government, and industry have a common goal: a city second to none in social, economic, government, environmental, and beautification as well as industrial development. The civic resident volunteer organization will be the heart of any city and have the knowledge and background to get the job done.

Section 3

The city civic resident volunteer organization will be staffed by highly qualified city residents. These motivated people will be led by:

- The city residents: forum council board of directors
- North, South, East and West resident forum councils
- North, South, East and West industry committees
- North, South, East and West social committees
- North, South, East and West economic committees
- North, South, East and West government committees
- North, South, East and West environmental committees
- North, South, East and West beautification committees

Amendment XV

Nations will divide their territory using basic economic principles.

Section 1

Economic Principles

Nations must divide their territories by economic principles rather than historic traditions. As an example, nations can organize states by providence or departments in specific natural areas, agricultural states, oil states, industrial states, tourist states, or financial districts.

This economic format will lead the departments or secretaries of agriculture, oil, energy, industry, tourism or finance to be the heads of these states. States, providences, and departments shall be divided by the same principles as the nations. The states will be structured with not more than three counties except for the larger states (large land mass) with four counties.

Section 2

Consolidate Government Institutions

This concept is designed to structure nations so they will fall in line with existing economic concepts in terms of direct responsibilities:

- By simplification and privatization, nations will save billions of dollars annually for taxpayers.
- This concept is designed to replace government's official *quantity* approach by *quality* in congress, state legislatures, counties, and city councils.

Amendment XVI

Division of governments from ideologies, conspiracies, or revolutions must occur in the name of "we the people."

Section 1

It is in the best interest of "we the people" and our government's efficiency at all levels to use the same policy as the industry counterpart. This means to be free of ideologies such as communism, fascism, socialism, liberal or conservative, family names, personalities, domestic and foreign interest with the intent of avoiding corruption, conspiracy or revolutions against our institutions in the name of "we the people."

Section 2

All nations, institutions, and the Charter of the United Nations will not conform or subscribe, under any circumstances, in their content or interpretation by any of the following terms:

- Executive powers
- Closed door meetings
- Special privileges
- Immunity
- Impeachment
- Ideologies
- Religions
- Racism
- National origin
- Government secrecy
- War powers
- Exile
- Discrimination/ reverse discrimination
- Campaign fund raising
- Interest groups
- Veto
- Loopholes
- Lobbying
- Political action committee (PAC)
- Public debts
- Seniority system jobs for life

- Debates controlled by parties dictatorship or multi party dictatorship government or special privileges
- Executive pardon

Section 3

Consequently, in the best interest of "we the people," our governments and institutions will not satisfy only the points of view of the homeless, poor, middle class, the rich, industry or the environmental movement.

Amendment XVII

Global Economy

- Continental financial integration.
- Standard economic principles apply to all nations.
- Balanced budgets - fiscal responsibilities.

Section 1

Continental Financial Integration

The United Nations economic council, along with another five economic continental councils, will standardize and require economic responsibilities in each continent. All nations will keep conservative economies in all regions and maintain a solid banking system. All nations will have a mandatory 100 year master plan and short term goals similar to that of industry.

Section 2

- Standard economic principles apply to all nations.
- Each continent will have a common currency.
- Each continent will have one central bank.

- All nations must have an efficient tax system.
- All countries must rank highly in the quality of its governmental policies.
- United Nations and continental economic councils will provide expert teams to assist nations to improve their financial operations.

Section 3

Balanced Budgets – Fiscal Responsibilities

The following budgets for the seven continents must be balanced at all times:

- Federal
- States
- Counties
- Cities

The heads of the United Nations, continental, Executive and Judicial branches, states, legislatures, districts, and cities will be directly accountable in maintaining fiscal responsibility. All budgets will be officially posted every quarter in the business section of all newspapers to be analyzed by "we the people." Public and foreign debt or mismanagement of public funds will be considered an act of treason against "we the people."

Section 4

The United Nations, Independent Political Science Advance Institute, and all continental economic public officials, industry leaders, and mass media will become familiar with all economic facets of the global open market. As a result, industry will be able to extend their businesses worldwide to reach billions of people.

Section 5

The United Nations shall have the power to enforce this article and exercise the appropriate majority vote in the United Nations General Assembly.

Amendment XVIII

Global Independent Commodities Agency

The responsibility of this agency is to monitor and maintain commodities at all times at stable and reasonable prices. The agency will represent the consumer, producers, industry, and the government. This consolidation of commodities will lead global industry to a reliable annual advance of the economic index indicator for future financial planning.

Section 2

A board of directors consisting of highly qualified men and women with extensive industrial backgrounds will structure the global independent commodities market. All 15 members of the board, three per each continent, will vote for the Chairman of the Board. In turn, he or she will select a secretary of the board.

Section 3

The United Nations shall have the power to enforce this article by the United Nations General Assembly majority vote.

Amendment XIX

Global Environmental Protection: "We the People" Environmental Manifesto

Section 1

The United Nations ministers in full general assembly recognize that the planet earth, as a whole, must be preserved at all times.

Section 2

The United Nations shall implement the following rules:

- Population must be contained within the nation's quotas.
- All nations' working hours must be standardized in all continents.
  - Working hours will be Monday through Friday, 40 hours per week, to improve planet earth with a Saturday and Sunday time to heal.
- All nations' governments will initiate flora and fauna restitution.
- Environmental 100 year master plans will be implemented and updated at election time to protect all rivers, lakes, air and land.
- The state, county, districts, city governments, and civic volunteer organizations shall have architects, leading landscaping managers, engineering, and technical personnel assigned to follow a specific blue print as a goal.
- Civil organizations will be encouraged to compete in the beautification of streets, boulevards, parking lots, beaches, fountains, parks, lakes, and rivers and take control of their territorial atmospheres.

Section 3

"We the people" will exercise our vote power through an independent research agency with constructive environmental ideas, suggestions, and solutions to improve the world, therefore, changing deserts, bodies of water, and the air at a rapid rate in order to live in a healthy world.

Section 4

Worldwide Environmental Report Card

The United Nations councils will issue a global environmental report card every quarter, six months, and at the end of the year to be published in all newspapers' business sections.

Section 5

World Court/United Nations Environmental Enforcement

- The nation's government shall implement all laws and fines.
- Industry that violates environmental international laws will be fined equal to 40% of the assets of the previous year's tax return.

World Court

Nations or industries that do not comply with the environmental international laws will be charged as public enemies of a crime against "we the people" and planet earth.

Section 6

The United Nations and all seven continental environmental councils shall have power to enforce this article.

Amendment XX

Space Exploration

Section 1

The United Nations space council's main objective is to monitor space exploration to be done for scientific benefits and peaceful means only.

Attention will be focused on the quality of the air status around the planet.

Section 2

World Funding for Space Exploration and an International Space Station

Seven continental space councils will equally finance scientific explorations in space and for the International Space Station.

Section 3

The United Nations, Organization of American States, European Union, Asian Union, Oceanic Union, and African Union shall have the power to enforce this article by appropriate legislation.

Amendment XXI

World Priority: Global Overpopulation

The biggest catastrophe socially, environmentally and industrially is caused by the world's excess population. We are six billion people and growing. Planet earth and world industry is only able to sustain a total population of 1.365 billion people as follows:

America	400,000,000
Europe	350,000,000
Asia	500,000,000
Oceana	15,000,000
Africa	100,000,000
Artic	0
Antarctic	0

Section 1

The United Nations Secretary General will introduce to the United Nations Assembly the world's "100 year population control master plan," updated at every election or every four years. The world's 100 year population control master plan will be reviewed by all confederations of nations as follows:

- Quota system applicable to all nations
- Encourage one child per family
- Education about global overpopulation implications in all schools will be required
- Heavy taxation of families with more than one child

Section 2

Present overpopulation increases poverty and depletes the resources of planet earth.

Section 3

The United Nations, continental multinational Secretary Generals, and the heads of each nation shall have the power to enforce these articles.

Amendment XXII

United Nations

Section 1

The United Nation's purpose is to:

- Keep harmony among nations
- Deal with almost any problem affecting humanity and planet earth

- Protect, defend, and enforce the Charter of the United Nations, Universal Declaration of Human Rights, and international democratic standards.

- Ensure equal rights for men and women

- Maintain international peace and security.

- Oversee all nations and balance all issues

- Lead to implement standards and common principles of government format in all nations

- Ensure all sovereign nations be ruled by democracy only

- Develop the United Nations "100 Year strategic master plan."

  - Once approved by the general assembly, councils will work directly with specific issues and be responsible for their success.

- Ensure all 194 nations' governments execute general elections according to the seal of approval of the United Nations, continental organizations and the 194 nations

- Restructure into a new updated United Nations organization where all councils will be directly working with specific issues and be responsible for their success.

The United Nations' Secretary General will be responsible for the success or failure of the United Nations. The Secretary General and councils will consist only of highly qualified best minds in the world people and elected by the general assembly.

Section 2

The United Nations' Secretary General, in order to perform his duties, will be assisted by the "United Nations Independent Research Agency" and the Secretary General assembly.

14 councils as follows:

- Security
- Social issues

- Economic
- Government and continental organizations
- Environmental scientific council
- Arctic and Antarctic Scientific
- Space
- Global military
- United Nations Political Science Advance Institute
- Peace keeping operations
- Global overpopulations and statistics
- World Court International Court of Justice
- Office of independent annual global town satellite forum meeting
- Office of independent scientific board of director's earth status

Section 3

Organizations or agencies not contemplated in the new United Nations format will be privatized. The other functions or detail work will be delegated to continental organizations and the 194 nations in the execution of social, economic, government, environmental, cultural and beautification issues.

Section 4

United Nations Budget

All 194 nations will finance the new United Nations format.

Section 5

Confederations of nations' chain of command:

- United Nations
- All continental organizations

Matters between nations on the continental level will be brought to the attention of the respective continental organization as indicated by:

- The Organization of American States
- The European Union
- The Asian Union
- The Oceanic Union
- The African Union
- The Arctic   U.N. Administration
- The Antarctic   U.N. Administration

Section 6

Continental Organizations

All continental organizations will operate under identical United Nations format.

Section 7

Continental Budgets

Nations will finance their respective continental organization.

Section 8

Continental organizations shall have the same Charter of the United Nations and the same functions, but be limited to the continent level.

Section 9

Nation's Standard Principles

Nations, states, providences, or departments, counties, districts, and cities will have standard principles and organizations.

Section 10

Global, continental, national, county, district, and city services all over the world will promote the standardization of government, industry, global economy and procedures. They will be under the same identical pattern. Services such as mail, traffic, area codes, zip codes, Internet and customs will be identical in all nations. Buildings, houses and streets will be in identical sequence in all cities or towns.

Section 11

The Collective Defense Treaty of the United Nations, Continental Organizations and Confederation of Nations
The nations' defense treaty is a mechanism that determines the status of a member. An act of aggression, domestic or foreign is considered an act of war against all other countries of that continent.

Guidelines:

In case of domestic or foreign acts of aggression, quarantine will be immediately initiated against the aggressor or nation responsible for the internal turmoil for the next 48 hours. Members of collective air, sea, and ground task forces, representing all nations, will take action. The United Nations will name an independent provisional government to take over. General elections in a six month time period under the new democratic format concept and standard principles will apply.

Section 12

The United Nations and continental organizations shall have the power to enforce these articles by appropriate general assembly majority rules.

Amendment XXIII

United Nations: The Democratic Project

Common Principles – Implementation

Section 1

"We the people" instruct the United Nations Secretary General and the existing confederations of nations to fully implement this democratic project.

Section 2

The United Nations' Secretary General will appoint a "United Nations International Standard Board of Director's Consultative Task Force."

Section 3

The United Nations' Secretary General will officially introduce to the United Nations General Assembly, the Global Peace Plan.

Section 4

The confederations of nations, continental multinational organizations, and the United Nations will implement the democratic project common procedures.

Section 5

The United Nations, Organization of American States, European Union, Asian Union, Oceanic Union, African Union, and the 194 confederations of nations shall have the power to enforce these articles in the name of "we the people."

International Democratic Standards on Global Justice and the World Court:

Worldwide Government Justice

Amendment XXIV

International Court of Justice
The World Court
The Hague
Netherlands

The World Court has jurisdiction about international cases among nations. The continental organizations and the United Nations already conform within the framework of the Charter of the United Nations and existing international treaties.

Section 1

"We the people " direct the World Court to ensure that all government officials and heads of state elected by their citizens be recognized as the only legitimate representatives of that nation before the United Nations, continental organizations and the confederations of nations.

Section 2

"We the people" instruct the World Court that any individual, group, political parties or any modality rising to power, either by force or in violation of international democratic standards will be on notice as having committed a despicable act of crime against civilization.

This charge, considered a "Crime Against Humanity," is in direct violation of basic rights in a civilized world and the Charter of the United Nations, the Organization of American States, the European Union, the African Union, the Asian Union, the Oceanic Union and the confederations of nations.

A criminal act against any nation and their citizens will constitute an open violation of already implemented international democratic standards and the Universal Declaration of Human Rights.

Section 3

Dictators and their accomplices will be required to appear before the World Court as is mandatory by international laws and be removed from power immediately.

Section 4

The United Nations, continental organizations, and the confederations of nations shall have the power to execute these articles in the name of "we the people."

International Court of Justice, the World Court, the Hague, and the Netherlands

"We the People"
The World Court

Versus:

- The illegal governments of the world
- All terrorist leader's organizations
- Illicit drug cartel leaders and their accomplices all over the world
- Piracy over the high seas

"We the people," by the power granted to us, as the ultimate rightful power in the world in our own universal constitutional inalienable rights, stand up in the defense of our civil liberties, our independence, and in the pursuit of *peace and prosperity* to all the human race, here ordain the World Court as their obligation and duty to begin proceedings against those individuals who have seized power illegitimately, terrorist organizations, and illicit drug cartels and must be tried for the following:

All unlawful representatives of governments, dictators as head of state, and their accomplices must be tried by the World Court for their roles in committing crimes against humanity. These crimes include harboring, training, and supporting terrorists and drug cartels in all continents in open infringement of the following international laws:

- Violation of the United Nations Charter
- Violation of the Universal Declaration of Human Rights
- Violation of international democratic standards

All leaders of terrorist organizations and their accomplices are responsible for actions humanity cannot allow. These are as follows:

- Serial killing of innocent men, women, and children in all continents by the use of car bombs, missiles, or guerrilla warfare on the continents of Africa, America, Asia, Europe and Oceania.
- Creating turmoil in the world by the destruction of hospitals, vital international oil supplies, airplanes and passengers, blasting bus stations, trains, schools, buildings, embassies, monuments, torturing and decapitating people, or killing United Nations peace keepers.
- Pursuing chemical, biological and nuclear capability to launch an attack on the civilized world.
- International intent to sabotage space satellites.
- Providing tainted food killing humans and animals.

All drug cartel leaders and their accomplices are charged with illicit drug trafficking with the purpose of destroying minds of innocent men and women.

- The distribution of illicit drugs all over the world has been the main cause of millions of people losing their lives.
- The civilized world, due to this human tragedy, has expended billions of dollars to help drug addicts.

- The world's annual cost to suppress drug distribution has cost billions of dollars.

Distress Global Political Legal Recovery Plan

A. The International Criminal Court for Criminal Justice shall have the power to enforce this universal rule of law within 90 days in the name of "we the people."

B. The World Court will make public a list of violators to the world and will issue the appropriate arrest warrants.

C. The United Nations, the Organization of American States, the European Union, the African Union, Asian Union, and the Oceanic Union will designate in their place a "United Nations Temporary Transitional Government" as the legitimate representatives of that nation to carry out governmental matters.

D. General elections will take place in 360 days under the seal of approval of the United Nations, the seven continental organizations, and the 194 confederations of nations.

The entire human race, acting in the best interest of all of us and planet earth will support the World Court in their efforts to bring to justice all of these criminals. The effort to legally convict those men acting in a mentally impaired manner to destroy civilization is by all means a step in the right direction.

The road to success is a *global human unified strategy* to put the weight of *global opinion* behind the World Court to put these despots out of business forever and sets out the global legal requirements that such assaults on nations will never happen again.

All of us six billion people, the worldwide political leaders, the religious leaders, the global free press along with the support of international human rights groups, "united we stand" to encourage the World Court panel of judges to start, without delay, the proceeding to make charges against all dictators, leaders of organized crimes against civilization, and illicit drugs cartel leaders.

The International World Court already has set a precedent in all aspects of these global litigations by convicting the president of Yugoslavia, Slobodan Milosevic, of war crimes in 1996 and in 2007. The court also issued an arrest warrant for Ahmed Muhammed Harum of Sudan with 51 charges of crimes against humanity.

Important Message to Humanity:

The Charter of the United Nations and standards for international laws provide severe criminal penalties for unauthorized individuals, groups, and their accomplices to assault any government of any nation by force or any other means to portray, or impersonate a legitimate government representative of that nation or their people. This criminal infringement of international laws will result in a charge of crimes against humanity.

"We the people," therefore appeal to the World Court, the supreme judge of the world, to start proceedings at the same time to all dictators and their accomplices to be charged with crimes against humanity and to place them in custody in the time frame of 90 business days. Accelerated actions will be taken to convict terrorists for the well being of humanity and planet earth.

A "global united we stand" strategy is required for success. It will be necessary for humanity to support the World Court in the complete elimination of these despots so these acts against mankind will not happen again. It is the duty and moral obligation of religious leaders, all political parties in the world, the global free press, and international human rights organizations to support the judges of the World Court to bring to justice and convict all such despots in the best interest of men and women all over the world.

"We the People"

Ordain the World Court supported by:

- The United Nations
- The Organization of American States
- The European Union
- The African Union
- The Asian Union
- The Oceanic Union
- Confederations of nations

The United Nations and the seven continental organizations will act immediately by law to provide a provisional government to conduct the administration of these governments in all aspects of economic, political, domestic, and foreign affairs of those nations with the rest of the civilized world. A time frame of 60 business days will be provided to conduct general elections under the seal of approval of the United Nations and the seven continental organizations, the World Court, the United Nations, and the confederations of nations. They shall have the power to enforce this resolution on behalf of "we the people."

- If by tomorrow all of the current 19 dictators were replaced by legitimate governments and freedom and human rights were observed by all nations, it will be a change for humanity of such a magnitude that has never before been seen in this world.
- All six billion people, united as one and not divided, with the main goal of "we the people, united we stand" policy can accomplish this goal by supporting the Global Peace Plan.

Global Suggestions

Constructive Solutions

Concerns

Observations

CHAPTER IV

THE SOLUTION:
THE MAKING OF THE TOP POLITICAL SUPPORT SYSTEM

- The Global Peace Plan, in a short period of time with five resolutions, will lead humanity from the worst to the best world class political organization the world has ever seen.

- If from the beginning of time man and woman had been equally balanced in the exercise of "voice and vote power" in a democratic format to direct their destiny, the history of humanity would be quite different.

- The statement that describes men and women at their best, "Give me a place to stand and I will move the world," was said by Archimedes (c. 287-212 B.C.) a Greek mathematician.

The Global Political Solution:

A matter of national and global securities and an assessment of humanity's struggle for a true democratic system

A View from the Top of the World

A global political point of view clearly indicates that the planet earth is facing the following two major problems:

A: Global Major Terror War Strategy is under way by a small dictatorial group of governments opposing, undermining, or disregarding present global calamities, by veto in the United Nations and by force opposing any initiative or agreement that leads to freedom, *peace and tranquility* in the world. Their political game is to wait until all democratic and advanced nations are weak because their people and political structures are so divided that such division will bring the balance of power in their favor. At that point they will emerge and openly launch a final and a massive attack on the space satellites of advanced Nations and begin urban guerrilla warfare at any place on earth they consider to represent their enemy.

B: Global Civilized Strategy

Important Notification to Civilization

There is no existing comprehensive "global alternative plan" by the present worldwide governments to prevent any scale of global terror war or any provision to defend and protect the sovereignty of the human race.

Alarming Global Political Report

This situation requires immediate attention of the present leaders of the most democratic nations in the world along with the Secretary General of the United Nations and continental Secretaries General to take steps forward to implement, without delay, the update of the present global democratic system to protect, defend, and enforce present agreements and international democratic standards as a universal rule of law.

In view of the fact that this lack of protection to the whole of humanity is of considerable importance, it is necessary that the following questions be considered prior to the implementation of such a global plan:

- Is this system providing for an independent task force to report every quarter the global political status of humanity, the

United Nations, the seven continents, and the confederations of nations?

- Is the whole political structure at the global, continental level and the confederation of 194 nations such that we shall have the policy "united we stand" when a nation or group of nations under dictatorships are in attack against civilization in violation of the universal rule of law?

- Will this system provide a socioeconomic governmental and industrial package to update all seven Continents?

- Will this system provide a center for the purpose of education in political science to government officials and their employees?

Important Requirement:

That this worldwide government democratic system will stand tall enough to protect, defend, and enforce the universal rule of law.

Global Political Open Letter

To: The heads of the most democratic nations in the world and the United Nations Secretary General
From: The civilized world

The President of the United States
The Premier of the United Kingdom
The Premier of Germany
The Premier of France
The Premier of Italy
The Premier of Canada
The Premier of India
The Premier of Japan
The Premier of Australia

Dear Sirs,

Humanity is calling on the United Nation's Secretary General and the representatives of the most traditional democratic nations in the world to lead a "global consultative task force. The objective of the task force is to take a decisive step forward to advance the present worldwide political establishment by building a prototype of a political organization that will bring the world's political future to a logical worldwide democratic government complex organization and produce the end of global political turmoil headed by dictatorial saboteurs.

The members of this consultative task force in turn will name a panel of seven members that will study the proposal for the Global Peace Plan; a viable five point solution to guide humanity and earth not only in achieving the objectives of the Global Peace Plan but to finish the job of the American and French Revolutions on a worldwide basis.

This Global Peace Plan will call for the implementation and resolution of the following five points to achieve that goal:

First	Activation of the global consultative task force initiative
Second	Implementation of a total global freedom plan
Third	Introduction of a worldwide government democratic complex
Fourth	Implementation of a Seven Continent's Major Recovery Master plan
Fifth	Creation of the United Nations' Political Science Advancement Institute

The Global Consultative Task Force Initiative

I. It will be a key to success and a job requirement that the "seven members task force" be chosen from among the most brilliant men and women in the world:

- Trustees of democratic thinking who will be open minded, goal oriented, of excellent character, and possess a high level of education
- Have an extensive resume of accomplishments in the private sector
- Excellent personality profile
- Be team oriented
- Have a capacity to get things done

Ideally, all members should be without preference or attachment to the present worldwide political establishment.

II. These members will study the five points of the Global Peace Plan for 90 days in a secluded university in the United States of America.

 III. They will write the five resolutions and the proper recommendations to the consultative task force which will in turn be given to the United Nations Secretary General.

IV. The United Nations Secretary General along with the heads of the continental organizations in a global town meeting with prime time news coverage will address mankind to announce that the Global Peace Plan will be implemented effective immediately.

V. Mankind along with continental organizations and the confederations of nations will declare that the land, space, and seas are created with the intent that freedom, and human rights will prevail. A global free press, the rule of law, and the exercise of checks and balances in all the governments in the world will flourish.

VI. Once approved by the United Nations, the Global Peace Plan will be in effect on a worldwide basis.

VII. All Nations, without exception, must align under the Charter of the United Nations, Universal Declaration of Human Rights, and the international democratic standards as a universal democratic system of values.

VIII. Non democratic governments will proceed to a peaceful transition of power to a United Nations provisional government which will be the legitimate government of that nation until general elections take place in 360 days conforming to the seal of approval by the United Nations and the seven continental organizations.

IX. The World Court will make a public list of the "Globally Most Wanted" and issue warrants to arrest dictators and their accomplices charged with multiple crimes against humanity who have become public enemies of the world.

X. As a precautionary assurance, all armed forces of freedom in the world will be on a standby basis in all continents and upon the seven seas.

XI. The global free press, television stations, news media, the Internet, and the entire human race will be working night and day setting the tone until the Global Peace Plan, with its five simple global resolutions of political agenda, is in place on all continents.

XII. A cease fire will take place all over the world. The terrorist and drug cartel organizations will be shut down and their people and their families required to report to the nearest city government centers where they will be held for job training.

The Highest Political Echelon in the World at the Global Level will be the United Nations and the World Court

The Continental Level consists of:

The Organization of American States
The European Union
The African Union

The Asian Union
The Oceanic Union
The Arctic   U.N. Administration
The Antarctic   U.N. Administration

The National Level consists of:

The confederations of the 194 nations

Political representatives of six billion people shall have the power to direct, instruct, and enforce the Global Peace Plan with recommendations from the United Nations.

From Humanity to all Levels of Governments:
The Global Peace Plan's Five Global Resolutions

I. Activation of the consultative task force initiative

Objective

- A consultative task force board of directors composed of the seven most brilliant and capable men and women in the world will analyze our present political format and the system and its five global resolutions.
- The board of directors will generate conclusions and specifics in a written document and their five resolutions to be presented to the consultative task force initiative in a 90 day frame time.
- This event will be highlighted and fully covered in a global forum town meeting with prime time news coverage.

Resolution

The United Nations, continental organizations, and the confederations of nations shall have the power to enforce this resolution by appropriate legislation in the name of humanity.

II. Implementation of the global total freedom plan

Objective

To pursue a "global united we stand policy" designed to alert the world that the concepts of democracy and "we the people" sovereignty have been obstructed anywhere in the world.

The intent of this resolution is very simple. It will end the threat to large or small nations by unscrupulous dictators and their accomplices seizing power in violation of major rules of the civilized world. This organized crime by the present 19 dictators, two drug cartels, and 41 guerrilla warfare groups is unacceptable. These dictators are not operating in the best interest of any nation. In fact, no rational person supports these people. The shocking behavior of individuals is nothing new; it has been going on since civilization began.

"We the people" cannot remain silent and ignore this calamity. There are real terrorists planning horrible crimes against their fellow innocent men, women, and children. These people have been threatening civilization before. They come and go leaving traces of misery everywhere. This time is different. The civilized world under democracy represents the largest organization and must confront the threat from such small groups.

This affects all levels of government. All six billion people intensely dislike such behavior that interrupts and sabotages the advancement of our civilization and ordains the following orders:

1. All elections must be approved unanimously by the United Nations and the seven continental organizations.
2. The United Nations and the continental organizations must provide a "transitory independent government" to allow a smooth transition into democratic government. A new constitution and the establishment of a new government elected by the people must be approved by all levels of government within 360 days.

3. All dictators and their accomplices must be relocated in 24 hours to another continent and forbidden any further involvement in political affairs.

4. Any deviation from these instructions will result in immediate global retaliation. Other sanctions will include weapons embargoes and freezing of assets for the crimes of illicit arms, drugs or guerrilla welfare. Anyone involved in terrorist activities will be subjected to the rule of law.

5. The World Court will charge crimes against humanity to all such violators and issue an order of arrest. Life in prison and other penalties will be up to the highest World Court to administer.

6. Such persons impersonating as heads of government will no longer be recognized as the legitimate representatives of their nation. All diplomatic and economic matters will be discontinued and immediately directed to a new provisional government selected by the United Nations and the Organization of American States, the European Union, the African Union, the Oceanic Union, and the Asian Union.

7. As a precautionary measure, all armed forces in the world will be in a state of alert to defend freedom and human rights.

8. Representatives of anarchy in any position civilian or military of any dictator of this type of regime will be declared persona non grata (unwelcome) and will be expelled from the United Nations, embassies, or any government agency in the world. A provisional government will be put in place immediately.

9. All levels of government will declare the entire planet earth to be under a "political global zero tolerance policy."

Global political "united we stand" and "zero tolerance policies" will be desirable instruments to all those who believe in freedom and democracy.

Resolution

The United Nations, World Court, continental organizations, and confederations of nations shall have the power to enforce these resolutions by appropriate legislation.

III. The "Worldwide Government Democratic Complex"

Objective

To implement, but not replace, the present worldwide governments based on a combination of democratic and economic principles capable of supporting a true democratic concept.

- All the elements are in place for redesigning the present global organizations to have a state of the art worldwide democratic government format that will stand the test of time.

The worldwide government democratic complex will have a format organized as follows:

Global Level:

- The United Nations
- Secretary General's Office
- 14 Councils
- U.N. Global Master Plan Office
- U.N. Global Humanity Center
- U.N. Natural Disaster Center

Continental Level:

- Secretary General's Office
- 14 Councils
- Continental Master Plan Office
- Continental Humanity Center

- Continental Disaster Center
- Arctic   U.N. Administration
- Antarctic   U.N. Administration

Important

Global and Continental Level:

a) Due to the size of planet earth, it is advisable for the global level and the continental levels to have identical political democratic organizations.

b) This arrangement will secure control and will make the management of the United Nations and the continental organizations more effective.

c) The flow of the worldwide political power will be a check and balance system under this *global political complex.*

The Confederations of 194 Nations:

Important

All nations and their people without exception will stand, protect, and defend:

a) The Charter of the United Nations

b) The Universal Declaration of Human Rights

c) The international democratic standards

d) Checks and balances in their own governments

Resolutions

The United Nations, the seven continental organizations and the confederations of nations on behalf of "we the people⊠ shall have the power to enforce these resolutions within 90 days.

IV. Implement a seven continent *major recovery master plan*

Objective

To present to humanity and the planet earth a practical and viable continental master plan to eradicate misery, ignorance, diseases, and bring all nations up to the highest administrative level of today's democratic and economic principles and to set forth a plan to restore the planet earth to the highest possible standards.

- This plan will allocate the amount of seven trillion dollars to restore all seven continents, their nations and the environment similar to the Marshal Plan that so successfully brought the European Continent to the level of peace and prosperity and one currency as it has today. This global effort to establish peace and prosperity in all continents is long overdue. Centuries of lack of attention have enabled constant sabotage by a gang of organized dictators assaulting society and our institutions.

- This plan will bring social, economic, and government managerial skills with a democratic format that will unlock our natural potential. It will focus on a pension and health care program that is affordable for all the poor and the middle class. Immigration will cease. People will go back to their mother countries to be with their own culture and their families. They will enjoy job opportunities under peace and tranquility in their own nation. It will provide schools, universities, decent roads, drinkable water, power, professional police, mail delivery, a communications system, industry that will produce jobs, a simple tax system and affordable housing. It will not only bring peace and prosperity, but will close the door forever to any attempt to produce organized terror, illicit drugs, or any assault on governments. Political turmoil will cease because all men and women will be free. No one will support such criminal behavior in any nation. It is so simple that the human race will finally enjoy a civilized world.

- Another explanation is that the concept of true democracy in all levels of government will satisfy all men and women on this planet. Government's officials and employees will finally work for "we the people" and the planet earth.

Resolution

The United Nations, continental organizations, the confederations of 194 nations on behalf of "we the people" shall have the power to enforce this resolution.

V. Create the "United Nations Political Science Advance Institute"

Objective:

The creation of a global political center will be used to teach our political representatives how to master the art of all aspects of a truly democratic worldwide government system and the care of our planet earth.

- The Institute will be staffed by the finest professors who have the capability to project a prototype of government for cities, districts, counties, states, nations, continental organizations and the United Nations used as an example to be emulated all over the world.

Universal Political Policy

"We the people," as the ultimate political authority in the democratic system recognize the democratic concept as our ideal; the inalienable rights as expressed in the United Nations Charter, Universal Declaration of Human Rights, and in international democratic standards. It will be, by all means, the policy of the Institute to build a democratic format that supports this concept all over the world.

Mission

The Institute's global curriculum will be oriented to be academically evenly balanced in support of the task to maintain humanity and planet earth under the care of the best trained and most brilliant men and women in the world.

Human Resources

- It will be the policy of the institute to maintain the highest job requirements for government officials and employees all over the political system. The same strategy will apply to their salaries which equal or exceed that paid in the industrial sector.

- The Institute will make public a worldwide *personnel manual* for government officials and public employees which will mandate the highest level of requirements to hold jobs in the government.

- It will be the policy of the entire political system to recognize that holding a job at any level in the government, anywhere in the seven continents, one must be up to the task of managing the most sensitive job in the world; overseeing humanity and the care of earth.

Worldwide Political Academic Studies

The Institute will divide their academic curriculum into two political faculties:

- Human Race Division
- Planet Earth Division

Human Race Division

This division will be managed to teach and research for humanity around the globe as follows:

- The Global Level
- The Continental Level

- The National Level

Planet Earth Division

This division will be managed to teach and research the world as follows:

- Air Preservation Authority
- Land Preservation Authority
- Water Preservation Authority

Global Level

This group will study and produce recommendations to improve the following organizations:

- The United Nations
- The World Court
- The U.N. 100 year master plan
- U.N. organizations
- U.N. documents
- U.N. Charter
- U.N. Universal Declaration of Human Rights and International Democratic Standards

Responsible to protect, defend, and enforce democracy as a universal system of values:

- U.N. "united we stand policy"
- U.N. "zero tolerance policy"
- U.N. annual report to the world every quarter

Continental Level

This level will study, research, and produce recommendations to improve the following organizations:

- Organization of American States
- European Union
- African Union
- Asian Union
- Oceanic Union
- Arctic   U.N. Administration
- Antarctic   U.N. Administration
- The continental 100 year master plan

Organized the same as the United Nations but at the continental level:

Continental Documents

- U.N. Charter
- U.N. Universal Declaration of Human Rights
- International Democratic Standards

Responsible to protect, defend, and enforce democracy as a universal system of values:

- Continental political organizations "united we stand policy"
- Continental zero tolerance policy
- Continental annual report to the continent every quarter

National Level

This level will study, research, and produce recommendations to improve the following organizations:

- Confederations of 194 nations
- Separation of powers
- The check and balance system
- Prototype of a nation as a pilot to be emulated in the world

National Documents:

- Nation's Constitution

Responsible to protect, defend and enforce democracy as a universal system of values:

- U.N. Charter
- U.N. Universal Declaration of Human Rights
- International Democratic Standards
- U.N. "united we stand policy"
- Nations "zero tolerance policy"

Report to their nation (every quarter just as in industry):

- Human resources job description:
    - The choice of the most accomplished people to hold positions in the government.

Introducing to all nations:

- Voice Power Democratic System
- Vote Power Democratic System

The master plan voice power office board of directors will be implemented by executive order. It will have a staff with a board of seven directors composed of only the most capable people.

a) A nation's 100 year master plan consists of long and short term goals for that country.

b) The nation's master plan office will prepare three versions of the 100 year master plan:

- plan A, plan B, or plan C

c) The nation's master plan office will make all three versions public at election time.

d) At election time, people will exercise their voice power by voting either plan A, plan B, or plan C.

e) The selected plan will be updated at election time if necessary.

f) All versions of the plan will be adjusted to the nation's budget.

g) The office will be independent and under no circumstances be controlled by the government administration.

Vote Power Democratic System

- The master plan vote office board of directors will be implemented by executive order.
- The office will be structured with seven board of directors selected from the most brilliant and capable people.

The functions of the offices under the Vote Power Democratic System will be:

The Office of Human Resources

- This office will produce a government human resources book which will contain a set of requirements necessary to qualify to hold jobs at any level in their country.

The Office of Federal Elections

- This office will be responsible for setting the time of elections which will be for the duration of four months, August 15 thru December 15, every four years. Only two consecutive terms are allowed by law.

Introducing Elections by the State/Election Method

- Each state or providence will present to the nation their candidates for president, congressmen, governor, and managers for districts, counties, and cities.

- All pre-qualified candidates will go to the primaries for a final debate which will occur on December 15 in a national mega election.

- "We the people" at election time will exercise voice and vote power by selecting plan A, plan B or plan C versions of the 100 year master plan and elect the candidates to do the job for the next four years.

Observations

- All levels of government will have their own 100 year master plan which will be goal oriented in the best interest globally, continentally, nationally, within districts, counties and cities.

- This system will stop the present worldwide government's vicious circle of interrupted long and short term programs of industries, agriculture, power, water supplies, education, pension plans, health care, senior citizens and the disabling of medical and medical prescription plans.

In Closing

The "United Nations Political Science Advance Institute" will have the responsibility to provide the world with the help of the greatest minds available to humanity and earth, the best ideas to improve, at an accelerated rate, development in the worldwide democratic complex.

Resolutions

"We the people" decided a long time ago that it will be in the best interest of humanity and the planet to have a superior education in political science. We believe that the "United Nations Political Science Advance Institute" will fulfill that need.

Therefore, the United Nations, the seven continental organizations, and the confederations of nations on behalf of "we the people" shall have the power to create the "United Nations Political Science Advance Institute."

Global Suggestions

Constructive Solutions

Observations

Concerns

CHAPTER V

THE IMPLEMENTATION:
THE GLOBAL PEACE PLAN

- "They can conquer who believe they can."- John Dryden (1631-1700)
- "We the people, united we stand" turn the tide to the side of the civilized world as a solid human chain around the world to show solidarity in our mutual interest to support the present political democratic leaders in order to implement the Global Peace Plan on all continents in 90 days.
- Men and women in the world will have incentives, peace, and prosperity secured by freedom and the rule of law.

The necessary task for mankind:
Global public service to perform

Our ancestors sacrificed their lives and their fortunes for the vision of a better life in this world and they did it under the most difficult of circumstances. One of these events took place in the 1700s when the American and French Revolutions were conceived to allow people all over the world to experience the ideal of democracy's concept of "government by the people."

It took more than two centuries to consolidate the present global political format. It is significant that today the largest and most powerful political organizations such as the United Nations, seven continental organizations, and the 194 confederations of nations embrace this ideal. While this achievement is as great as it appears, it is in need of the urgent attention of every man and women in the world.

Mankind has a Public Service to Perform

We are close to mastering great political success that will bring peace and prosperity to the world. However, we have a few men and their accomplices who are determined to inflict damage and destroy this ideal so they can control and destroy our civilized world. We can no longer ignore the present vast satanic global conspiracy. This treacherous situation will exist as long as we tolerate it.

Mankind's choices are very simple:

1. World Tragedy

A divided humanity will continue with major World Wars until we destroy ourselves and our planet.

2. Peace and Prosperity NOW

A cohesive humanity implementing the Global Peace Plan will bring peace and prosperity.

We have come a long way since the opening of the United Nations in October, 1945. We are on our way to achieving what was unthinkable at that time. Today we have the potential to establish a worldwide government democratic complex.

- We have to use our ingenuity and fight force with intellect.
- Humanity has to stand up and fight for its rights.

It will be in our best interest at this crucial time that we put our own personal political interests aside for a good common cause. The cause is the unfinished business of the French and American Revolutions to form a great society on this planet so we can enjoy it along with freedom and the rule of law.

Objective

The main purpose of this plan is very simple. It consists of an arrangement of a "global unified civilized front" to support our worldwide political system by sending a clear signal that "we the people" will fully support the implementation of the Global Peace Plan in order to finish the task of the American and French revolutions on a world wide basis in a short period of time.

A Global Unified Civilized Political Support System:

The Global Peace Plan calls on:

- Humanity
- Women of the world
- All religions of the world
- Global free press

The Global Peace Plan calls on these groups to cooperate in the same manner as when a major natural disaster challenges us. With the same kind of determination as we acknowledge and present the ideal "united we stand," we will have to organize our thoughts in a logical way to avert a possible escalation to World War III as the present saboteurs of our global political system intend and plan to do. If this is ignored, as we have seen in the past, it will eventually lead to a global war.

- The global political situation requires the use of all actions at the civilized world's disposal. This political response cannot be limited or confined to a single nation or group of nations; on the contrary, it has to be a combined effort and responsibility so that all the requirements of total freedom on a global level are united and are met by humanity, men and women of the world, our religious leaders, and the global free press.

- The key to success is to exert the full influence of "global opinion" to support the United Nations, the World Court, the continental organizations, and the confederations of nations to implement the Global Peace Plan in a 90 day time frame.

- The civilized balance of power is in place and is on our side.

- Six billion people have a common denominator of a unified goal based on freedom, human rights, and the law of decency. We cannot ignore this basic instinct. Our ancestors contributed their fortunes and their lives to leave a legacy of ideals that would change the way of thinking in all corners of the globe.

Today these ideals are contained in articles of the Charter of the United Nations and the Universal Declaration of Human Rights. They are also in all continental charters and all nations' constitutions as a universal rule of law waiting to be defended, protected, and enforced by people all over the world.

- "We the people" today are aware of all aspects of our civil rights and what we have as our resources in the way of instant communication so we no longer live in total isolation.

- "We the people," must support the Global Peace Plan because at the present time the political situation is so dangerous. It is time to inform all political leaders of the free world that we must move forward with this plan.

The great global society officially instructs, directs, and demands the United Nations, the World Court, seven continental organizations, and the 194 confederations of nations to proceed without delay to the implementation of the Global Peace Plan within a 90 day time frame.

A Public Letter to Humanity

Ours ancestors set the foundations for a universal democratic system of values with the intent that governments will flourish and expand these principles to secure a better world. Today, advanced nations and their citizens accept and set an example of how freedom and the rule of law can bring peace and prosperity. Mankind has the global political organizations in place based on those same principles and ideals to form a g*lobal political advancement system of nations.*

The final conclusion of the American and French Revolutions projects has been maliciously undermined and sabotaged for the last two hundred years by a small band of dictators with very disturbing, shocking, and obsolete ideas that adversely affect the foundations of all the continents, nations and their institutions. Humanity has built a vast global political system to stop the present vast conspiracy.

The Global Peace Plan's agenda has the capability of ending this malicious cycle; it is now up to mankind to regulate the political system from the worst to the best political organization in the world. There are people at the present time living under illegitimate regimes. If they are ignored by the free world as in the past, it will set a serious precedent to the human race.

The preservation of freedom is the right of all of us and must not to be confined or limited to a region or continent as it is an irrevocable and indisputable natural universal rule of law.

A Global Strategic Master Plan for Worldwide Freedom

Objective

"We the people" will initiate the global freedom operation with the intent and only purpose to bring the whole weight of world opinion by the voice power of humanity to demand and instruct our legitimate political representatives to defend and protect the Charter of the United Nations, the Universal Declaration of Human Rights and the International democratic standards as the only legal instruments to protect the sovereignty of all citizens in the world.

- This unified course of action should be supported by all of us is with the sole purpose to end war as an element to resolve political problems on all continents.

- The Global Peace Plan defines a valuable option with straight forward simple resolutions to bring peace and prosperity in the world.

A Public Letter to All Women in the World

Women make up the majority of people in the world. Mother Nature's indisputable laws dictate that men and women have a profound place in all decision making in all aspects on this planet. This combined effort will bring a more suitable balance to fight force with intellect and get results by peaceful means in the present global political scene.

It is urgent that this force become active to bring a well overdue equality between both sexes as a vital and important strategic course of action to implement global peace and prosperity in a short period of time. For the most part it has been men, rather than women, who have been active in the political arena. Men have used force as a tool to fight force resulting in a painful and slow process that has taken more than two centuries with no end to it to the point one of them is recognized as the bloodiest century in history.

If from the beginning of time, men and women equally balanced the exercise of "voice and vote power" in a true democratic format to direct their destiny, the history of humanity would be quite different. We have seen the present escalating global insurgency for the last 15 years, illicit criminal drug traffic for the last 40 years, the bombing of cities, and groups terrorizing the civilized world since 1989.

During the last few years, we have seen airliners used as ballistic missiles, trains, restaurants and churches blown up, the killing and torturing of members of the free press, as well as nuclear threats by an 'axis of evil.' The disruption of the global economy has occurred by the systematic bombing of oil pipelines which suppressed the oil flow with the purpose of disrupting the Global Economy causing global prices of goods to rise. What is more incredible, are the groups claiming responsibility and openly taking credit for this criminal psychopathic behavior.

All of this makes it necessary to join forces at all global levels under a new political policy composed of a "global united front." All men and women of the world, as well as the present legitimated governments, democratic representatives headed by the highest echelon of the United Nations, the seven continental organizations and the 194 nations demand the consideration of consolidation of civilized forces due to a mutual interest. Clearly, democracy is in a state of "Red Alert" until all the Global Peace Plan's requirements are met.

Present generations face the last vestiges of the Dark Ages calamity controlled by a few men and their accomplices. They take over nations posing as representatives of their citizens and using their resources in the name of religious ideologies, nationalism, and other excuses to suppress men and women to the degree of degradation. These 19 people, the worst dictators, get behind a veil to promote global insurgency using our ("we, the people") money to buy arms and tactical equipment. They support and harbor accomplices who are hired to kill people who stand in their way.

Objective

1. The objective of such people is to prevent this worldwide democratic complex from reaching its potential to build a system that will satisfy the poor, the middle class, the rich, industry, the government, and the environment.

2. Under a new political policy "a global united front," all men and women of the world call upon all the present legitimate government representatives, the heads of the highest echelon of the United Nations, the seven continental organizations, and 194 nations demanding the immediate global priority to put the entire "worldwide government complex" in a state of red alert until the global peace agenda is implemented.

Public Letter to All Religious Leaders and Members in the World

"We the people" must address all religions in the world with the objective and only intent to enlist their aid to work together with all six billion people to finish building a total civilized government system that will satisfy all points of view.

This planet is our home. We come here to grow, get along with the rest of the world, get an education, have a job or business, have children and grandchildren, and live the rest of our lives enjoying our golden years.

This simple way of life in the civilized world has been interrupted by crisis and tragic events of major proportions which affect our way of life. This situation, caused by small illegitimate governments that impose terror, has always existed since the Dark Ages. These harmful people not only sabotage our economy, free society and its institutions, but use religion, ideologies and myths. In fact, they will do anything legal or illegal to remain in power. We are now past two millennium of continual conflict affecting all of us. This shocking behavior has got to stop.

It can no longer be found acceptable for the following reason:

- Due to the advancement of technology in the production of arms we can no longer afford to play war games without risking and endangering civilization and the planet's support system.

"We the people," in view of this grave situation, must request the present leaders of religious groups to ask all their members around the world to participate in the "global forum town meeting" that advocates to:

1. Join the civilized world and not support this vast global insurgency so all military and civilian people can return home and be reunited with their families and let the political world system run legitimate governments by a universal rule of law.

2. Send the word to our political leaders in the United Nations, the seven continental organizations, and the 194 nations to expedite the Global Peace Plan to help people around the world in 90 days.

Our ancestors gave us fundamental principles of freedom that set in motion today's global system of government which is still used to the advantage of large and small nations. This world must be safe for all of us or no one will be safe. This violence can no longer be tolerated. Our struggle for freedom and the pursuit of happiness is long overdue. Your contribution in these matters will prevail and will be a cornerstone in the future of all men and women all over the world.

A Public Letter to the Global Free Press

To the newspapers, radio stations, television stations, magazines, the movie industry, publishers, writers, the intellectual foundations/institutions, Internet of the world, ladies and gentleman of the world:

As we review the last 2000 years, we must be aware of our tragic political history and the present crisis just beginning at the new millennium. This is considered an era of the greatest turmoil and tragedy ever known to man. It has left us to believe that this global terrorism and insurgency is, without question, the most barbaric form of criminal behavior since the Dark Ages. If this situation remains unchecked it will eventually lead to war. In a sense, we have seen in the 2000s a preview of World War III. There is no question that our way of life, our civilizations, and institutions are in great danger. The faceless enemies who promote this treacherous behavior are very clear about their purpose.

Mankind has formed its own opinion and understands that in order for an immediate form of collective defense by all the people, our global, continental organizations, and the confederations of nations that legitimately represent democracy must regroup behind a new strategic alternative option: the Global Peace Plan. This is composed of new

103

revolutionary solutions that provide in a short period of time, without loss of life, a new era of freedom and prosperity.

"We the people" call upon the entire world to put an end to a legacy of the last 2000 years of tragic events and be certain that this time the world will never again experience this type of political atrocity. "We the people" request and invite the global mass media to join all men, women, and religious leaders of the world to unite in support of the Global Peace Plan.

The Greatest Global Political Machine

Global Positive Political Educational Message:

In order to change our way of life from daily shocking, destructive news to a "worldwide democratic complex" that satisfies the poor, the middle class, the rich, the government, industry, and the planet earth's needs, we must form as one united by freedom and the rule of international laws and our own nation's constitution as a common denominator. Humanity has to admit that all of us have committed a terrible global tactical error that brought the global wars. At this point we consider the political situation an advanced chronic disease that has to be cured.

Presenting a New and Effective Global Plan for World Peace

I. "United We Stand Global Front" Policy

Objective

The strategy will consist of mobilizing the civilized world to form a "united we stand global front" policy with the intent and only purpose to send a clear signal to the United Nations, the World Court, the continental organizations and the confederations of nations that humanity must support, demand, and instruct our entire political system to put into operation the Global Peace Plan.

The strategy is to have men and women, religious leaders, and the global free press as united forces around the world, ready to use their initiative and ingenuity in a more advanced proposal of human solidarity; to advance peace plans in a strong united front.

Humanity Political Contract

This contract states that all men and women, religious leaders, the global free press and all resources of the civilized world solidified under a universal agreement, the "united we stand" policy, to establish a "political common sense world order" within the present worldwide democratic government complex.

"We the people," the present worldwide democratic complex represented by the United Nations, the World Court , the Organizations Of American States, the European Union, the African Union, the Oceanic Union, the Asian Union, the Arctic, Antarctic continents and the confederations of nations in order to determine a more beneficial relationship among the parties recommend the following:

Article 1

Humanity and the "present global political establishment" recognize that the past and present human calamities and frustrations serve as lessons in the seeking of peace and prosperity. The imposing of ideologies, religious, dictatorial form of governments, personalities and other unexplained reasons have resulted in shocking daily crimes against humanity.

Article 2

To consider that in order to form a bond and better understanding, both parties involved must resolve to end this political human tragedy.

Article 3

The Global Peace Plan will serve as an expedited way to reach that goal in 90 days by consent, using five simple resolutions that will lead to the finest organization in the world. The United Nations, the World Court, the seven continental organizations and the confederations of nations will justify their existence by establishing a world political system of checks and balances in all our government institutions.

Article 4

All present political documentation - the United Nations Charter, the Universal Declaration of Human Rights and international democratic standards already approved by humanity will be observed, protected, and implemented to provide sovereignty for all men and women everywhere in the world.

Article 5

This upgraded political system will not tolerate public officials and political parties endangering their nations by placing their ambitions above the welfare of their government.

Article 6

Dealing with dictators:

Terrorist organizations and illegal drugs cartels will collapse and be repudiated by humanity and the present government worldwide democratic governments. Instead, a global political zero tolerance system will be reinstated that will stand the test of time.

Article 7

A cease fire will occur all over the world. All nations will provide their own professional forces which will secure domestic democratic tranquility.

Article 8

The Global Peace Plan, as a major global strategic policy, will be in existence in 90 days time through the United Nations, World Court, continental organizations, and the confederations of nations.

Article 9

The entire political system shall protect, defend, and enforce these articles in the name of humanity.

II. The Power of Instant Communication

Objective

To spread the voice that the time has come that both freedom and human rights be heard in all nations and continents and to let it be the new basis to build a great human society.

The technologies that are available today can now allow anyone anywhere to easily send a straight forward notice, to all existent levels of governments that this political turning point is in the best interest of all men and women all over the world.

Humanity has been seeking the way to a "better world" for a long time. But now, with the ability to have instant communications, we can have all sectors of the world to turn the best of our abilities to focus and concentrate all the power vested in all of us to guide the United Nations, the World Court and the entire political complex to end this cycle of madness all over the world.

This is an opportunity of a lifetime. We have in place all the global political organizations, the present political officials, government employees, the financial support, the instant communication, and most importantly, finally "we the people" have a plan, the Global Peace

Plan. This will turn around the political substandard government organizations from the worst to the finest organizations in the world.

It is time "we the people" face the fact that this vast political organization is on hold simply due to a chain of errors committed by our political leaders and employees. Just take a look at the past horrible total global wars and regional conflicts to see that the lesson that needs to be learned is not to simply win the war, but instead to set the notion and the necessary reassurances that these atrocious crimes against humanity never happen again.

We must understand today that globalization has brought us into another dimension in our way of thinking that what is good for humanity is good for the United Nations, the Organization of American States, the European Union, the African Union, the Asian Union, the Oceanic Union, the Arctic and Antarctic continents and all 194 nations of the world.

The entire global mass media must send a constant daily educational lecture to our political system that the time has come to implement the Global Peace Plan. Humanity calls to all men and women, who bring us the news day after day that being united, not divided, in the political issues will eventually lead to peace and prosperity. We have the tools of the Internet, e-mail, cell phones, phones, 1-800 numbers, fax machines, magazines, newspapers, radio, and television stations which are all available around the world ready to be used in this freedom journey.

The global mass media, by simply building the moment and the tone, will move the *global opinion* as one to support an upgrading of the present worldwide democratic government. The keys to success are to:

- Glamorize democracy, the Charter of the United Nations, the Universal Declaration of Human Rights, and international democratic standards as the rule of law in all nations.

- Evict dictators, terrorist organizations and the drug cartels from the face of the earth as the significant cause of all our calamities for the last 200 years.

- Serve warrants by the World Court to all 19 present dictators, their accomplices, international terrorist organizations, and drug cartels that have committed crimes against civilization.

- Implement a new era where industry, economies, and the political world will work united for a new democratic ideal in all nations.

- Upgrade the United Nations, continental organizations and the confederations of nations to be able to carryout the policies to protect, defend and enforce present world documents. The democratic standards all over the world already signed by all nations as a requirement to be a member of the United Nations and the continental organizations will be enforced.

- Immediately cease fire all over the world.

- Immediately return home all troops, the coalition forces, NATO forces, and the United Nations peace keepers to be replaced by professional military forces that will defend freedom and human rights of their own democratic nations.

The civilized world's intention and only objective is not in any way to conquer or subject nations large or small to any culture or control. On the contrary, it is a system based on universal international democratic values that warrant the sovereignty of all men and women in the world.

III. Access to the Present Political Establishment Objective

To facilitate the access to our present world wide governments we must officially introduce the Global Peace Plan to:

- The United Nations
- The World Court
- Secretary Generals

- The Organization of American States
- The seven continental organizations
- The heads of 194 nations
- The head of the congress or parliament in all nations
- The head of justice of all nations
- State, district, county, and city public officials
- All consulates
- All foundations and universities
- All major religions in the world
- All forms of mass media

Human Race Incentives

- Once implemented, the Global Peace Plan will bring about a peaceful life for all.
- History books will close the chapters about the fear of aggression and war forever.
- Men and women will have equal rights all over the world.
- The upgraded worldwide political system will focus on protecting and defending all people as it enforces the universal rules of law.
- All points of view will be satisfied by this new political system which will require the United Nations, continental and all national organizations to use the short term and long term master plans of their own to bring about a major recovery.
- The United Nations, the World Court, the continental organizations, and the confederations of nations will be run even better than the private sector.
- Global economies and their industries will be equally balanced and strongly diversified in all continents as trading currencies of exchange are consolidated into five currencies, one per continent.

- The "United Nations Political Science Advance Institute" will provide the best ideas on how to run successful governments at all levels when based on democratic and economic principles.

- Education, pension plans, health care, housing, senior citizen plans, and all services such as: mail, communications, roads, water, and power will be studied by the best minds in the world to provide humanity with quality services.

- The planet earth, as the main support system of life, will be a primary concern to be maintained by the scientific authorities in this field.

- The press, movie industries, television stations, cartoons, radio, newspapers, and magazines will enjoy freedom of expression all over the world by sending constructive messages, telling only the truth, with solid common sense. Freedom will be glamorized as a universal system of values. We are not all wired the same and people need reminders in all communication dimensions to do the right thing. Above all we need to be proud of our countries and be part of the beautiful planet Earth. We need to simply live in a civilized world.

- Exiles and masses of displaced people from all over the world will be able to return to their homeland with their families so they may make contributions toward their prosperity and that of their nation.

- The Global Peace Plan subscribes to the idea of the prevalence of logical and rational concepts as far as economic and democratic principles are concerned.

The conclusion is that poor judgment by political leaders in the United Nations, continental organizations, and heads of states and their political parties has put their ambitions above the welfare of the worldwide democratic political complex.

"We the people," until now, have ignored what happens in the rest of the world, and have accepted time after time to live in a global political inferno ignited over and over by a series of dictators and their companion global terrorist organizations.

"We the people," due to the present global calamity and for our own well being and the preservation of our planet as our only support system, must initiate the Global Peace Plan without delay.

OBSERVATIONS

It is up to the United Nations and the continental political representatives such as the Organization of American States, the seven continental organizations and territories, to protect, defend and enforce the worldwide international democratic standards.

- Nations will set in motion their own master plan with long and short term goals that will be suitable for them and for their citizens. The plans will be realistic and able to be maintained and complete within themselves and with the rest of the confederations of nations.

- Freedom, universal human rights, and economic opportunities will allow the natural human strength of mind to be a contender as a revolutionary force that will shape humanity.

- The global economy calls for 7 trillion dollars to go to each continent and will be known as the "Continental Recovery Plan." This will be a powerful incentive to induce humanity to support this plan.

In Closing

Distress signals were initiated in the late 1990s. By that time, political leaders of the civilized world tried to regroup all nations into a global common cause of government but this action failed and the opportunity to have a unified system of freedom was lost. It was another one of history's turning points which led to careless mistakes by allowing the proliferation of another generation composed of the worst dictators who make up the chaos we are experiencing today. Some nations decided to proceed and live in the free world by joining the confederations of nations and others have joined at the continental level. They have formed the European Union and are able to live under freedom and the rule of law which has brought about a unified currency, the Euro, as its legal tender.

Millions of people in substandard nations are forced to live under inefficient and dysfunctional systems. Today some countries live under the worst scenario as these countries are left entirely in the control of totalitarian dictators. These nations and their millions of innocent people were abandoned by the civilized world.

This constitutes an inexcusable act of betrayal of billions of people living in the civilized world. The global free press and the high level echelons of the United Nations, their institutions, the continental organizations and the confederations of nations not only failed to do their job but failed to meet their moral obligations.

Eventually this large mass of the global population lacking freedom and human rights came under a totalitarian system which affected their economy and industry. It gave them no chance for a future. This allowed them to be easy targets for unscrupulous political leaders as they took advantage of people by making false promises and by revolting against the free world in the name of ideologies, religions, and myths. In reality, the sole purpose of the unscrupulous political leaders is to remain in power for life.

If a political situation of this magnitude is sustained and neglected as in the past, the whole civilized world, the global free press and political organizations like the United Nations and the seven continental organizations in the present democratic format will fail. When this occurs, the unscrupulous political leaders will accuse the advanced nations of being responsible for the rise of insurgency. This will lead to chaos brought on by suffering due to hunger and the lack of the basic needs of life which will result in a state of frustration.

The civilized world, on its own, will have to become the leader to see that this present global insurgency is stopped or more dark times are on the horizon and cannot be ignored. As time goes by, we will be unable to stop the global insurgency as it gains control. This is not a complex or impossible task. Nothing in this world will divert our will. If we unite against the 'Axis of Evil' we will prevail.

It is not rational to support these criminals or their accomplices. The greater part of the world detests these people who will not hesitate to blow up the whole world or to create fear using oil and illicit drugs to control and intimidate. It is in our best interest to evict these 19 dictators. This task of freeing our fellow human beings is significant and compares to the monumental task that our ancestors faced.

Freedom, Universal Declaration of Human Rights, and the observances of the Charter of the United Nations – "We the people" should be our main concern.

Our future is well defined and the decision rests with all of us, to act for the good cause of a universal declaration of freedom. It is up to the present generation to complete the ideals that were started by the American and French revolutions more than two centuries ago. People born in other nations will have the opportunity to return to their homeland if they so desire, and will still partake of economic advantages of what is now known as "the free world." This will help strengthen all those presently living in underdeveloped countries.

The End

Global Suggestions

Constructive Solutions

Observations

Concerns

ABOUT THE AUTHOR

Ricardo Osorio, Sr. combines his experience as a military officer, diplomat, and businessman as the author of the Global Peace Plan with the belief that conflicts, suffering, poverty and sub-standard political organizations throughout the world can be eliminated.

This book is the key towards a realistic new plan to bring peace and prosperity in the World.

The Global Peace Plan is enlightening and uplifting in a profoundly different way and offers a simplified solution that will result in a better way of life for all us.